To the
FREEMASONS
and OTHER
VERSES

To the
FREEMASONS
and OTHER
VERSES

ROBIN ELLIOTT

authorHOUSE®

AuthorHouse™ UK
1663 Liberty Drive
Bloomington, IN 47403 USA
www.authorhouse.co.uk
Phone: 0800.197.4150

Published by AuthorHouse 05/13/2015

ISBN: 978-1-5049-4254-6 (sc)
ISBN: 978-1-5049-4255-3 (hc)
ISBN: 978-1-5049-4256-0 (e)

Print information available on the last page.

Contents

Intoduction to Poems...xv

A blank page 1
A lone star...2
A market town in Autumn...2
A new generation..3
A night of despair...3
A Simple Conversation...4
A small life...4
A temporary day 5
A Tranquil Morning 5
A voice of dissent..6
A Vow...6
Abracadabra..7
Accept our apologies..7
Accidents happen..8
Adored One...8
Air travel..9
Air 9
Alan Turing 10
Alcohol 11
Aliens... 12
America.. 12
An Approximation of Sanity 13
An insult to modernity 13
An optimist's suicide.. 14
An unmown corner 14
Another day of sun and sin and sensation............................ 15
Anti-social secret tribe 15
Are We Free to Act Unconventionally.................................... 16
Are You Enjoying the Weather? 16
Artists and craftsmen.. 17

As sane as the next man.. 17

As the zoomblat plays 18

The Auction of Time 18

August Bank Holiday 19

Avebury 2013... 19

Awake at night 20

Babylon... 20

Balls of space 21

Barricade my door 21

Benevolence 22

Blackbirds 22

Boiled Eggs... 23

Born again cynic... 23

Born Again Lover... 24

Bring wild words... 24

Burdened down by Mum and Dad 25

But still tomorrow... 26

Butterflies... 27

Canute can't 28

Carlos 28

Christmas is over 29

Christmas 29

Come dine with me 30

Come here.. 30

Counting Magpies.. 31

Cut flowers 31

D.N.A. 31

Dandelion 32

Decay 32

Deceive to Deceive 33

December sunset 33

Deliver me from eternal death...................................... 33

Dignity Escapes Notice 34

Divinity Rages 34

Dog.. 34

Drunken thoughts... 35

Early morning rain 35

Elvis is dead 35

English Beer... 36

Enjoy me 36

Entangled Apes 37

Envy the young 37

Eric Satie 37

Eye contact 38

Eye to Eye 38

Fallen Water 39

Family hang ups abound 39

Fire 40

Foreign booze 41

Foul Masonic scum 41

Free Gas 42

Freemasonry 42

Friendly fire 42

Frost 43

God is doubting you 43

Half an Hour 43

Hang on in there 44

Happy today 44

Home 44

Houses 45

Howard 45

Hurtling towards death 46

I am a lunatic 47

I Am Acting Aimlessly 47

I am hearing voices 48

I'm no white settler 48

I am not me 49

I am sufficiently conscious 49

I blame my parents for what I am 50

I buried your body 51

I can tell you I love you 51

I didn't believe it 52

I don't know what will happen next 52

I live gladly 53

I love you 53

I miss being me 54

I Record the Mind 54

I remember yesterday 54

I Send My Message..55

I sympathise with Oscar Wilde 55

I think I've lost my mind..56

I Wake 57

I Write Love..57

If I Heard Voices 57

If You Could Read Between the Lines 58

If Your God Gave You All You Wanted 58

Illicit thoughts 58

I'm gonna shit on you 59

I'm great 59

Immortal lines..59

Imperfect Bodies 60

In the silence of the night.......................................60

In the shadow of the church 61

Infinity Beyond Infinity 61

Irish Hymns..61

Its only ink..62

It's Raining 62

Jerusalem...63

John Hampden..63

Jupiter 64

Late night music 65

Leave me alone 66

Let me live 66

Let the trees grow old 66

Lie-bore scandal 67

Life and death..68

Life nags 69

Like a lamb to the slaughter 70

Live now before times final call...............................70

Live simply now..71

Locked In...72

London..72

Lost in the crowd..73

Love thy neighbour 73

Market day in England 73

Masonic Bullies..74

Masonic bums 74

Mervyn Peake...75
Momentum, supremacy..76
Mortality..77
My line lives on...78
My Mind Will Change 78
Night time..79
Night...79
Nightmares 80
No place to stand upright..80
Notes for a Final Poem 81
Nothing has a purpose 81
Nothing much happened today 82
November 2..83
November...84
Now Is Wow...84
NZ Poem 85
October Girl 85
Old farts of England 86
Old..86
On this day I lived and loved 87
Ouvret la porte 87
Pass the Time 87
Payback...88
People Watching 88
Picnic..88
Play on..89
Poetry..89
Pottery...90
Prepare to fly 90
Provence provides...91
Rain beats on speckled glass...91
Ray..92
Red and yellow 92
Retirement..93
Right Now 93
Running on Empty..93
Sadness is impossible 94
Sectioned 94
Sedition has been made easier...94

Self portrait with loathing 95
Separate from the Voodoo 95
Shakespeare 96
Silence the whistle blowers.. 96
Sitting doing nothing 97
Sleep creeps 97
Smokey's art is sublime 97
Snoring for England 98
Snow 98
Solomons Decision.. 99
Someone to love... 99
Space time is mine 100
Spanish coffee... 101
Spanish Holaday.. 101
Spring...102
Suck Justice from the Sky 102
Summer Bees...103
Summer dawn..103
Summer Rain 104
Summer Sun...104
Sunshine gives you cancer 105
Swallow the sky..105
Symbolism stops at my door 106
Tall trees grow here..106
The Tap Drips...107
Tell God what to think..107
The A.A..107
The abandoned village 108
The Adjacent Man..108
The age of reason has passed us by 109
The angels of solace 109
Pottery..109
The Asylum 110
The Average Delinquent 110
The barbecue... 111
The beautiful survivor... 111
The Big Apple...112
The bigwigs are bending 112
The birds of the air stand bedraggled....................................113

The Black People..113
The blank page...113
The bookcase... 114
The cause.. 114
The chicken liberation front...115
The clowns of celebrity 115
The Coming party.. 116
The crazy years of age 116
The daisies are humble. 117
The daisies dance with litter 117
The Dawn.. 117
The devious county councillors... 118
The distant window 118
The dream 119
The drunken roundhead.. 119
The egg in the nest 120
The electric vigil 120
The final couplet.. 121
The Fireball 121
The freedom of madness.. 122
The funeral in the rain... 122
The Funeral... 123
The future explodes... 123
The Game of Musical Standing...124
The Garden...124
The gentleman of Rotary...125
The God who doesn't exist..125
The Greek Tragedy 125
The hall of echoes...126
The heart of Brighton 126
The home-town blues...127
The injected life..128
The Irish know, (on reading Ship of Fools)...................................128
The Irish Mug..129
The jack of speed no.2 129
The jackdaws chatter 129
The Jazz of Diversity 130
The jewellery of the sky...130
The king of number 23..131

The knock on the door...132

The Last Cuckoo...132

The Law of the Exceptional..133

The lemmings 133

The lottery of life 134

The Lovesong of Tomorrow..134

The Lunatic Screams 134

The M.P.s of Buckinghamshire...135

The Madhouse Killer..135

The minute 136

The moment of elation 136

The moment of flight 137

The moon 137

The mother of parliaments 138

The Music has stopped..138

The N.H.S. 138

The new day 139

Nightmares...139

The Notes of Satisfaction..140

The Olympic Flame..140

The open door...140

The orchid in the woods 141

The pan fried dead 141

The past burns in 142

The Past...142

The Photograph...142

The poet of unparliamentary language 143

The portrait 143

The Practical Pacifist..144

The Racing Mind..144

The Rain Falls 144

The rain 145

The Red Lion..145

The resistance 146

The riot in the library 146

The Rose..147

The sentences of now 147

The Sign at the Entrance...148

The sky promises 148

The Son of a Hero...149

The song of summer's coming 149

The sorrow of silence...149

The triumph of sound...150

The speaker of the house of commons................................150

The statue of liberty 150

The sun is shining now...151

The sun sets in the north 151

The testimonial of esteem 152

The thieves of the mind 152

The tide in the marshes 152

The tyranny of consultants 153

The victims of psychiatry..153

The village on the hill 154

The voice of Tina Turner 154

The vortex of the night...155

The way home 155

The Whisper..156

The Wind in The Ashes...156

The wind in the willows again..156

The wordsmith's fate 157

The yaffle 157

The art of pottery 158

They think their God is better...158

Thick trousers...159

This poem...159

The average minnow rampant 159

Throw caution to the wind 160

Tibet...160

To David Jason and Jackie Stewart 160

To Dine With Children..161

To Hate a Stranger...161

To live on..161

To Ray 162

To Ray 162

To Read or Write 163

To see you bastards gone 163

To the freemasons..164

To Tommy and Pat 164

To William 165
Today is now 165
Today the sky is dry 165
Today's earth 166
Turn off the lights 166
Two hours after midnight 167
Uni-verse 167
Unparliamentary language 167
Vegetable companions 168
Verse... 168
Waiting for the dawn 169
Washing the car and mowing the lawn................................ 170
Wat Tyler and John Bull 171
Waves, flames and clouds. 171
We are truly blessed 172
What bollocks... 172
What do I need today... 173
What Do the Birds Do... 173
What I thought in the womb 174
When Black hates White.. 174
Whitney Died 174
Who is reading my words... 175
Winter fruit 175
Wiser than myself 176
Wishes... 176
With W.B. To Innisfree 177
Without Me 178
Woman's hour 179
Women's Boxing.. 179
Words are free 180
Write on... 180
X 180
You are no brother of mine... 181
You took me in my diluted sanity 181
Your love is all 182

Intoduction to Poems

This is what I leave behind. A loose arrangement of words which I hope will convince my children that the stream of consciousness in my mind was more than a puddle of piss steaming into oblivion.

A blank page

A blank page
And no idea.
A fearful task
On this lonely night.

A blank page
And no idea.
I wonder what
The hand will write.

A blank page
And no idea.
An onerous task
At first sight.

A blank page
And no idea.
A demanding challenge
For the hand of sleight.

A blank page
And no idea.
A fearful task
On this lonely night.

A blank page
And no idea.
I wonder what
The hand will write.

A lone star

A lone star
Shines in its velux cradle.
Guiding me to my dreams and a night of sleep.
Starlight from another world
Pierces the misting glass.
A winter sun
Many millions of miles away
Glints in.
White light that has travelled
To the earth for many years
Falls softly on the blinking eye of slumber.
Lone star shine down
And caress me in my nest
My guardian on this cold and wintry night.

A market town in Autumn

A market town in autumn
Busies itself before the coming winter.
Yellow leaves
Remember a lost summer now fading
As shoppers scurry before an October wind.
A leaden sky hangs heavy with circling cloud.
In the High Street the traffic splashes in guttered puddles.
The barrow boys in the Market Square call out
The fate of the last cabbages and caulis.

A new generation

The sound of children's laughter
Rings down from the future
You are opening the door on a new generation.
This is your purpose.
Love the young.

A night of despair

If you would only commit
To a night of despair
You would see
That you are dead now.

Don't waiver at the door
It's all gone.
Tin pot hope is betrayed.
There is no more.

Yours Sincerely
The deceased.

P.S. Goodbye

A Simple Conversation

A simple conversation
Can save a man from oppression
To chew the fat
About the weather
Or the economy
Can steady the mind.
It reminds us
That we should love our foes
And our fellow man.
Positive company can redeem.

A small life

A small life
Lived in simplicity
Is what you had.
You never asked for more.

Quiet days
Lived in domesticity
Were yours.
Why ask for grandeur
When happiness is available with less.

A temporary day

The world turns on.
Eastenders broadcast after granny's death.
And as the homeless walk the streets
The T.V. churns.

Seemingly there is no end to earth
But short life burns.
Man sees his days pass
And bows to time.

A temporary day is all.

A Tranquil Morning

A tranquil morning
After a good nights sleep
Offers the hope of a new day.
The slate clean
The mind refreshed
Its time to begin again.
The life I wished for
May be about to begin.

A voice of dissent

A voice of dissent
Can be heard amongst the crowd
Speaking truth in constant isolation.
Who will listen to the small lone voice of honesty
As the self-deluding herd carry on.
Bring an end to Britons caste system
Free the untouchables.
Share the wealth of the nation out to one and all.
The privilege of the craft is an abomination.
With the masons in charge Briton sucks.

A Vow

The game of negotiation
Is life's staple.
I offer you everything
Please accept.

Abracadabra

Abracadabra,
This is magic.
The quickness of the mind deceives the eye.
I told you I was deceptive.
Don't believe a word.
Every sentence contains a lie.

Accept our apologies

I face the trauma
Unaware that my appointment with fate has been missed.
The doctor will see you now.
Sugar pills for the dying.
This is the placebo.
I am sorry you have suffered
But our hands were tied.
We regret your coming death
But the dice were loaded.
Accept our apologies.

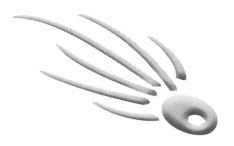

Accidents happen

A life cut short
With a car's crashing.
There's one less teenager in the world tonight.
The parent's lament.
If only we hadn't lent her the car.
Overtaking on a bend
She felt the lorry's force.
Blood spilt and the hospital form read D.O.A.
The wreckage blocked the road
As the ambulance carried the limp corpse away;
To be no more in this world.
Accidents happen.

Adored One

Adored one   I wait in anticipation
Come to the door   Confused by music

Air travel

The cramped seat and packaged food say air travel.
Six hours of mind-dead boredom till journeys end.
A foreign jaunt begins, the time unravels,
With only a gin and tonic for a friend.

Air

A breeze of disturbed air
Runs through my hair
And reminds me
That all is change
And even the wind must wane.

Soft contact from blown gases
Says that all is well.
The atmosphere dances
And the sweet breathe of life
Fills the lungs.

Blades of grass bow
As their surroundings shift.
Oxygen lives.
The transparent zephyr of life
Moves again.

Alan Turing

In Alan Turing's mathematical mind
There sat an enigma.
The brain that shortened the war
And saved a million lives
Was taken to gay doom.
The police of Manchester
With the laws of the day
Ruined the genius of England.
Hormonal suicide cut short a brilliant life.
The state's shame still hangs in the air.
You can't apologise to the dead.

Alcohol

Crazy days of alcohol
Determine the lives of many.
Unable to resist
Or admit to a surfeit
The addicted drink on.

The mind is fogged
And the pocket emptied.
Bad health and confusion steal the day.
The liver scars
And violence abounds.

The bottle is no friend.
No thirst is worth the consequences of dependence.
No liquid lunch is worthy of a life's demise.
Imbibe at will and satisfy the craving
And feel enslaving drink choke the brain.

Aliens

Many billions of stars shine
In far flung galaxies
Where the aliens brood in solitude
And the U.F.O.s are for free.

As the universe expands they wonder,
Is it further to earth today
Millions of light years just for a visit
And space craft just don't pay.

The little green men are jealous
They're lost in outer space
They're trying to keep up with the neighbours
And they're missing the human race.

So send up the U.S.S. Enterprise
And give the klingons a call
There only as far as the most distant star
And the chances are bugger all.

America

Today America, the land of the free.
Will the patriots call ring true in the travellers mind.
A thousand Atlantic miles till journeys end.
Fly west silver Boeing to the New York dawn.
We will visit the masters of the world
And gauge their worth.

An Approximation of Sanity

This is my best approximation of sanity.
Are you impressed?
I seek to convince you
That I'm worthy of approval and freedom.

An insult to modernity

The masons are to simple to see their own guilt
They believe that they are righteous
United in their collective delusion
They patronise the state.

Their separate minds and pervasive deceit
Are an insult to modernity
Who needs the bunkum of secrecy
In the 21st century?

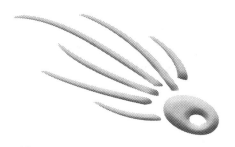

An optimist's suicide

The first signs of failure are showing.
Don't panic.
This is normal.

The end is obvious.
The fabric will descend
And chaos will ensue.

It's time to reassess.
An optimist's suicide
Is no cause for despair.

An unmown corner

In an unmown corner stands the bladder campion,
Successor to the celandine
And neighbour to wild arum.
In this, the garden's abandoned portion,
The flowers of the wayside thrive and bloom;
The seeds of the wild world germinate and set.
Brambles creep along the fence
And nettles flourish in unkempt patches.
Hedge woundwort lifts its purple petals
And ivy climbs the trunk of a sapling ash.
Here natural life has its space
And survives without the aid of man.
Here independent species find repose.

Another day of sun and sin and sensation

The sun creeps its slanting morning shadows
Through opened curtains and across the illuminated floor
The light of the coming day spills onto a waiting wall.
A trees outline is silhouetted on the warming plaster.
The heat of the coming day begins its climb;
From the rising sun the yellow dawn begins.
Bring me another day of life
Another day of sun and sin and sensation.

Anti-social secret tribe

Anti-social secret tribe
Not communicating with the plebs
Can you give justice
In silence?

The maxim of the law is
Justice must be seen to be done.
Not handed down as a fait accompli
By a secret society.

Are We Free to Act Unconventionally

Are we free to act unconventionally
To change our shoes for no reason
To take medication without supervision
To dance naked in the gutter.

What control is there
Over the easy riders.
What lock can hold
The legitimate mind.

Are we free to be obtuse
Free to live and not harm our fellow man
But merely challenge their prejudices.
Are we free to harm a fly?

Are You Enjoying the Weather?

Are you enjoying the weather
Its an unexceptional grey day
A perfect day for living
In between the sun and rain
We breathe in the clouds of the heart.

Artists and craftsmen

Artists and craftsmen,
The creators of beauty and innovation,
Fight with the outrage of madness and poverty.
Divorce and lack of money pursue them.
They are harried by the bank manager and the taxman.
The price of artistic integrity
Is loneliness and ridicule.
The individuality and strength required to stand alone
Is the muses demand.
The studio of arts endeavour is the home of the brave.
Fame and fortune evade the many.
The struggle for existence is the norm.

As sane as the next man.

I am ready to leave the asylum.
Leave it for the madhouse of society.
The streets are full of the uncertified
Queueing for a chance to espouse their superstition and irrationality.
Judged by fools I declare
I am as sane as the next man.

As the zoomblat plays

As the zoomblat plays
The kneebee sways.
All dinkly were the hobby groves
As the twinklies crimbled o'er.
Beware the fencrition.
This is pastitution.

Tomorrow brings reknoblification
And the trembly toves.
They bind in grimlitude
If sarafication isn't forthcoming.
Oh resound the drumblies!
All is terribleeding.

The Auction of Time

Fleeting youth has deserted me
I age by the day
I have no time to stare at the clock
No hours to waste.
In the auction of time's dispersement
I bid with what I have left.

August Bank Holiday

The rain beats on the conservatory roof
Rhythmically pounding out the music of the deluge.
Another surge of the torrent brings a fiercer sound.
Enough water to wash away the sins of a year
Bursts from the gutters.

The air is full of drops of water
Soaking the sodden earth.
A months rain in an hour brings renewal to the grass.
The day trippers feel the Bank Holiday blues
But the weather is answerable to nobody.

Avebury 2013

Where stone age man dug and hued
To create a monument to his gods,
Today the tourists pass
In anoraks of red and purple.
A thousand generations of crows
Have picked these stones
As time has worn the ancient henge smooth.
In the car park the married couples argue
As the stones imperturbably look on.
What was dug for centuries
With antler picks and woven baskets
Lives on in the twenty-first century
For tourism.

Awake at night

Awake at night
Watching the clock
As the digital display
Counts out the minutes
Of endless time.
The waking nightmare of masonic abuse
Prevents sleep.
How dare you bastards?
How dare you?

Babylon

They double your medication in Babylon hospital.
If you don't get better they blame your mind.
The cause of psychosis is other people.
Sort them out and I'll be all right.

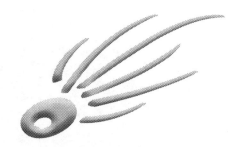

Balls of space

The rhythm of the planet
Runs in accord with the sun and moon
Our partners in the old Newtonian dance.
Seasons surge as the solar system moves.
The birds and trees live by its embracing law.
The ocean tides bring the lunar news.
The balls of space spin on.

Day follows night around the turning globe
Rotation brings light and warmth to end the dark.
The rites of man, his ablutions and his work,
Are received from the passing rites of space.
The movement of the heavens is earth's steady clock
Till stellar doom ends it all in the final night.
Meanwhile the balls of space spin on.

Barricade my door

In hours of solitude
A feminine malice of control
Makes darkness longer.
Barricade my door for I may go mad
If your lies are thought to be true.

Benevolence

If the silence is to be broken
Would you hope
That the noise that filled the void
Would be benevolent?

Blackbirds

The blackbirds engage in hopping wars
Marking out their territory.
The chase, the fight, the sparring battle
See the new intruder flee.

Preparing for the coming spring
They stamp out their destiny.
This is mine. Come no further.
I am the king of the Linden tree.

With nests to come and spring song too
They prepare for what is to be.
Frightening off the young pretenders
And putting on a show for me.

Boiled Eggs

The shattered shells of boiled eggs
Recall three minutes in boiling water,
Soldiers dunked in the yellow excess,
The morning begun with foods exacting promise.

Toasted bread, the staff of new life,
Is cut by the silvered knife.
Breakfast begins a new day,
The chicken's sacrifice is the fuel to start again.

The yolk stains the cup,
The spoon cradles the albumen in white.
Simple pleasures raise the heart
To face the daily strain.

Born again cynic

I'm a born again cynic,
I worship in a church of my own.
I know the price of everything
And the value of a pound.

I am not trustworthy.
I may take a bribe and still not play ball.
What you sow is what you reap
And I have stolen the seed.

Born Again Lover

I am a born again lover
On this amorous day
Rejuvenated by your smile
Living in the prosaic aftermath of splendour
Knowing that we were together
In golden moments.

Bring wild words

Bring wild words
To the ancient ruin of my life.
I devour the night.
It is the prelude to another day.
Life's opportunity to beneficially exist.
Run riot in the blessed hours of privacy;
There are no witnesses to this insanity.
The doors are locked
I am myself.

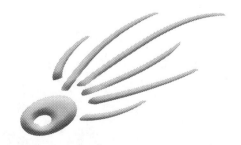

Burdened down by Mum and Dad

Burdened down by Ma and Pa
I hear you say
You regret that you listened.

What they expected
Was not what you wanted.

A litany of criticism
Was the accompaniment to youth.

They dragged you down
With relative disapproval.

You can't choose your parents
But you should have chosen to ignore them.
Ma and Pa were fallible.

But still tomorrow

What have I learnt from sixty years?
Try to say cheers
When you are bought a drink
And think
Before you criticise.
Everyone is tired of disapproval
And the removal
Of one more hassle
Is a battle
To be savoured.
Time passes
Times change
But there's nought so strange
As continuation.
Still here
Drinking small beer
And dreaming.
Time to regret
And yet
No sorrows.
The past's a mess
Lived under duress
But still
Tomorrow.

Butterflies

By the nettles and the weeds
Fly the butterflies
Living their brief lives
In the sunshine of today.
They mate and die
And pass the hours of their existence
In fluttering exuberance.
The colour of their wings
A natural beauty for the eye.
Atop the thistle and the scabious
The suction of the proboscis gives them nourishment.
Their summer lives soon over
They seize the bright days of July
Before they pass away.

Canute can't

Hold back the tide
Can Canute.
Canute can't.
The tide won't stop for him.
Wave goodbye to sovereignty.
Surf is up.

Hold back the tide.
Aching groynes
They can't.
The tide is free.
The moon's journeyman.
Beating the shore.
Forever more.

Carlos

Carlos
Inspire me once again.
I call on Santana
To speak my cause
Six strings of excellence
And the percussion of heaven
Express my views.
I remember Woodstock
I remember Wembley
I remember Birmingham.
Fill my head with love.

Christmas is over

Christmas is over
It's time for the January grind.
Winter days and winter nights bring gloom
And soon the wind and rain.
And still the chill.

The clouds pile up in the Atlantic
Queueing to burst over England.
Leafless timber fills the woods.
Wild animals struggle to live out the freeze.
The wind howls in the trees.
No birds sing.
Draw the curtains and wait for spring.

Christmas

The Christmas of a child's delight
Is remembered fondly
But what of other times
When families argued
And the moody threats of hatred
Led to the divorce court.
I see to be this way
Another day
Is what is coming.
Prepare for the season of goodwill
And prepare for the families end.

Come dine with me

If you could repeat the love you showed me
I would be happy again.
Our date at the restaurant
Was a meal with an angel.
Come dine with me
Your presence is sublime.

Come here

Come here
Gonna dissolve you in saliva.
Generous diva
This is armageddon.
I'm a getting my way.
My bodily fluids are staging a take over.
Ain't semen strange.
This is me.

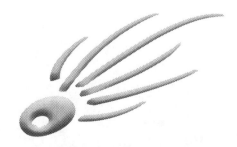

Counting Magpies

I'm sitting in the garden counting magpies.
If they don't come in pairs I shoot them.

Cut flowers

Pinks and dahlias stand upon their fresh cut stems
In a sunlit, transparent, engraved glass vase.
The petals offer floral colour
And the temporary beauty of their brief life.
The lower stem sunk in discoloured,tepid water
The blooms held high in windless air,
This symbol of love
Will fade before the month is out.
The captive flowers will wither and die
Before the love of their owner
Has had time to follow suit.
The bouquet, an amorous gift from an ardent partners heart,
Will know the death
That separates and ends all of loves endeavours.

D.N.A.

The battle for the grandson's mind
Is being waged in England.
Will the spiral carvings of his D.N.A.
Save him from oblivion.

Dandelion

Dandelion dance and sway in the breeze,
Tease the air with your sinuous bending.
Send seeds from your summer clock
Across the gardens of suburbia.

A bullfinch feeds on the threadbare head
Plucking a meal from the plant.
The splendour of nature's moment is all.
In a flash of red it goes.

Decay

Lives of upright probity can end in alcoholism
This is reality.
The clash of expectation and life.
Do you believe in virtue?
No idle thoughts will save you.
Sure purity will lead us all stray.
The belief in the goodness of mankind
Collides with actual people
And the debris hurts.
Expectation of better days
Leads to disappointment.
Those perfect babies
Become flawed arguing men and women.
That new marriage becomes tired and faded.
The middle aged and middle class
See their dreams turn soar
Unless they can still love and tolerate.
The only hope is to embrace the imperfect
And accept what you are given.

Deceive to Deceive

Deceive to deceive
The truth will do us good
Don't fight the word
The word is.

December sunset

Orange clouds spill from a December sunset
Swirling water vapour fleeing the chill winter wind.
Ochre edged shapes splashed with grey and white
Fit for a masters brush and a canvas recollection.

The western horizon is lit with ribbons of flaring fire
A gamboge hue defies the coming night.
The impending darkness squeezes the straining light.
An hour of beauty is the suns departing prize.

Deliver me from eternal death

Plastic flags fly high
As the dirty rascal apologises for his existence.
Summer afternoons slip by.
The stork imbibes in independence.
Applaud the new
It's time the driver stopped.
Take a leap into the red.
Piggy puddles are in the box.
Despondent junipers sway.
Deliver me from eternal death.

Dignity Escapes Notice

Dignity escapes notice
As the madmen fart.
They smell their own odour
And complain.
Negative to the core
They are pustules of animus.
Their brains fried with the garbage of false brotherhood
They exhale nausea.

Divinity Rages

Divinity rages
In my natural, not supernatural, soulless mind.
I swear at the ceiling.
Four dead in Ohio
Tin soldiers and Nixon
Still lives in my mind.
This is the ascent of man.

Dog

Loyal dog sleep by my feet
And spend the day in bonded friendship.
Let man's hunting comrade
Rest his canine body.
There is no companion beyond a dog.
A heart of honest kinship
Is sweet rover's gift.

Drunken thoughts

A clear mind sees that all is wrong
And alcohol dispels the myth.
Blurred thoughts are better than some.
The ache of reality is best dissolved by wine.

A blurred mind sees that all is wrong
And wine dissolves the truth.
Drunken thoughts are better than none.
The source of reality is best dispersed by wine.

A distilled mind sees that all is wrong
And time disturbs the truth.
Alcoholic thoughts are better than none.
The reality of now is best ingested with wine.

Early morning rain

Early morning rain beats on the roof,
The gutter runs and the downpipe gurgles.
The English moan
But this is what stops the Home Counties becoming the Sahara.

Elvis is dead

Collect your thoughts
And post them in a letter.
Elvis suggests you return them to the sender
But he is dead.

English Beer

English beer pulled from the pump
Into the embossed glass tankard
Passes the lips and travels through the throat
On its way to the drinkers brain.

The brewer's creation, the pint of pleasure
Brings welcome liquid relief.
Sup from the glass and swallow the ale
This pub is England's glory.

Enjoy me

This morning we are separated
By seven miles of road, fields and hedges.
I write surrounded by the madhouse walls
And rules.
I compose my love song.

To you I owe it all.
My recovery and my happiness.
And my new chance in life.
Another kiss awaits.
A life of sex and sunshine beckons.
On this the first day in September
I declare
I love you.
Enjoy me.

Entangled Apes

What was ecstacy for us
Was just a stolen moment
For two entangled apes
Circling the nearest star.

Envy the young

I long for the days of youth
When first love crossed the meadow of my life.
I long for the first time that philosophy touched my path
And I foolishly thought I was to be the equal of Erasmus or Aristotle.
I long for the moment I realised my life was just beginning
Before I realised it was almost gone.
I yearn for the century passed
When technology was a benevolent friend
And the digital age was just a dream.
To be young was a perfect vision
The future awaited like an unbroken promise.
Age takes its toll on all flesh
There is no option but to envy the young.

Eric Satie

Eric Satie
I stood at your door
and watched womankind enter.
Your acerbic mind
and distilled music
carry me back to Montmartre
where the artists play in the sunshine.

Eye contact

Charles is looking shifty,
Rogers face is twitching,
Mark is trying to look away
Stephen is trying too hard.

Let me introduce you to the cast of bad actors
The people who give their secrets away
By failing to make proper eye contact
And living a dubious lie.

Eye to Eye

Can you see eye to eye with a fool
A fool you don't even want to see at all
And agree to virtual insanity.
Cyberspace will break the lunacy
There are no secrets in the age of the internet.
You can't silence justice.

Fallen Water

On this grey day
The sky hangs heavy
From horizon to horizon.
The saturated air
Is motionless with limp humidity.
Leaves drip and bear the drops of fallen water.
The darkened earth lies still.
The boundary fence is striped with sodden patches.
Snails come out to celebrate their luck.
This summers day
No one will see the sun
It lies hidden behind the June-time veil
Of all embracing cloud.

Family hang ups abound

Family hang ups abound.
What we did to each other
Reverberates down the years.
Divorce and estrangement
Follow each other
As the children regret their past.

How can we forgive the perpetrators of old crimes?
Can love survive betrayal?
Parents abuse the youth.
And youth disregards their begetters.
Mother dear you screwed me up
And now I've done it to the kids.

Fire

The fire burns
In the ash-strewn hearth
As the blackened grate grows hot.
Winter's chill is repelled
Throw on another log.

Flames dance
And smoke curls.
The air receives the warmth.
Outside the wind blows
Take shelter from the storm.

Orange tongues
Discuss in crackling tones
The coming of the heat.
The glow of conflagration
Lights the room.

Billets of wood
Surrender and become ash.
As evening becomes night
The chimney carries away
The signal of combustion.

Smoke swirls and rises
Darkened bricks support the mantel
In flickering light
The shadows play
Throw on another log.

Foreign booze

Far away in a foreign bar
Immersed in foreign booze
The language is strange
And the currency is a farce.
The beer tastes of holidays
And the food is all meat.
The taxis are a rip-off
And the waitress has seen it all before.
Auf wiedersehen, au revoir, ciao.
Have another drink and have it now.

Foul Masonic scum

Foul Masonic scum of Tindal,
Hippocratic hypocrites
Cover up the disgusting truth with your unprofessional lies.

Slaves to the royal scam
Persecute an innocent man
I have no delusions about my lose of liberty.

Break free from the septic eye
The twisted lies of the immoral tribe
I loath the lodge and the ways of untruth and perversion.

Falsehood fills the mind of fools
A community that breaks the rules
Roll up your trouser leg and give us a thrill.

Inject me with lies and make me ill
Give me the bitter tasting pill
England would be better to see you bastards gone.

Free Gas

Breathe deeply,
Suck in the air.
This gas is free.

Freemasonry

In a world of backstabbing deviants
There is no place for honesty.
You must lie with the liars
And twist morality.

There is no hope of a clean life
No hope of telling the truth
The mind's sewer is open
Perversion rules the roost.

Friendly fire

I'm stressed and struggling
Under pressure
Dodging the bullets
Of friendly fire.

I'm regrouping,
Putting up resistance
Waging a war
For my hearts desire.

Frost

The dawn reveals a frost ;
Clinging whiteness waiting for the sun.
The lawn is sugar coated with frozen frills
As the December cold takes its freezing grip.

The church roof tiles are patterned.
The north side in a shadows chilling thrall.
The coming day will melt winter's ice
After the chill dark of night will come the thaw.

God is doubting you

This is no illuminated manuscript
No monks embellish these words
The margins carry no medieval pictures
It is the blunt truth.
God is doubting you
Play dice with God.
Einstein at the speed of light sits on the bookcase
The potters have made clayhenge
The actors put on a dumbshow
Sun sun will deliver.

Half an Hour

How much relaxation can you fit into half an hour?
How much mania can you fit into half an hour?
How much being can you fit into half an hour?
How much love can you fit into half an hour?

Hang on in there

Hang on in there,
Better times are coming.
The future will bring wisdom
And a true companion.

The days that are left will be positively charged
As the clocks roll on to old age.
Seize the day and enjoy the moment.
Your one and only life is up for grabs.

Happy today

Happy today is all you can ask for.
Tomorrow you may be dead or double crossed.
The expectations of an optimist are likely to come apart.
Cling to the wreckage and hope.

Home

Sell the old home
Where family memories abound.
Move on with ruthless momentum.
There is no place for sentimentality
In real estate.

The places where the children played
Are worth money.
The room where lovers vowed
Are available for finance.
This pile of bricks is an agents dream.
For 2% they will dispose of your life.

Houses

The houses stand as their occupants pass through,
The human tide dwells only for a while.
Bricks and mortar last for generations
Flesh and blood dies young and fills the grave.

No. 53 saw children turn to adults
And parents age to senility and beyond.
No 42 saw beloved granddad die
And his widow fade to aged skin and bone.

The builders leave their legacy in lines
Streets of house counting out our days.
The Tudor and Victorian live on
As man goes on his brief and short-lived way.

The streets see the turning centuries pass
Their fashions and their music come and go
Children inherit brick and tile and glass
For sale signs mark the peoples passing show.

Howard

The weak and wiry legs walk on.
The white, hollow cheeked face looks out.
Clothes hang limply from the skeletal frame.
Cancer consumes the body, eats the flesh.
The final days approach.
Ravaged by disease, Howard drinks.
The bitter taste of death in each new pint.

Hurtling towards death

When I was young
Time seemed unending
And the possibilities of life
Seemed unending too.

Now age has made me
A shadow of myself
And time has worn a pathway
Through my heart.

Each new ache
Brings an awareness of ageing
I am time's slave
Edging towards decrepitude with each new day.

The passing hours
Slip by in nostalgia's wake.
The bloom of youth
Has worn out its temporary sheen.

Forgive my dismay.
I thought there was more.
Hurtling towards death
I record my mindful sorrow.

I am a lunatic

The moon shines bright on this autumnal evening
Lighting the dark as the electric glow diminishes.
The sky that prehistoric man saw
Is mine tonight.
The moon will outlive Armstrong.
It will circle til doomsday
Turning the tide of our dreams.
I am a lunatic.
Glad to see the months fulfilled
And the phases turn again.

I Am Acting Aimlessly

I am acting aimlessly
Relaxed and chilled.
I don't care what I write next
I'm in the zone.
In the groove
And that's enough.

Words will say what they want
When they want.
A sentence will appear.
Now I celebrate contentment.
Type what you will
The word is willing.

I am hearing voices

I am hearing voices
The voices of doves
Crying in the darkness
For a world that hates itself.

I'm no white settler

Like the U.S. Cavalry
Under John Wayne
You rode to the rescue
And lifted the siege.

The Cherokees are beaten
They've fled to the hills
The wagon trains rolling
The fort is relieved.

But never forget
I'm with the Indians
I am no white settler
These are my beliefs.

I am not me

Dementia fries the brain.
' I am not what I was ' says granny.
The shell of a personality lives on.

' I forget who I am.' 'Who are you.'
In a home for the elderly they survive
Asking the questions posed by an emptying mind.

I have forgotten my name.
I no longer remember my day.
I am not myself.

I am strangely vacant.
I am a fading memory.
I am not me.

I am sufficiently conscious

I am sufficiently conscious
To know that I am enjoying myself.
But as there are few alcoholics with happy wives
I know that this boozy day
Must not become the norm.
The warmth of the marital bed
Requires more than moments of sobriety
To fuel the blessed fire.

I blame my parents for what I am

I blame my parents for what I am.
It's not my fault at all.
I blame both Ma and Pa
For my descent and my fall.

I blame them for my problems
And my lack of success in life.
I blame them for their lack of love
And letting me choose such an awful wife.

I blame them for how my kids turned out
And the fact that I'm in debt
I blame them for letting me of control
Without a safety net.

I blame them for my drinking
And my run ins with the law
I blame them for my money woes
And how I have become poor.

I blame them for my dodgy genes
And what they let me be
I blame them for the very fact
That they were just like me.

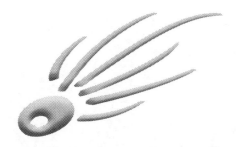

I buried your body

I buried your body as honour bound
Where the four winds met.
I planted the cross
To mark the falling of a knight on foreign soil.
There was no memorial to fallen valour
No mourning crowd to mark a saint in opprobrium.
Let sneering time be you remembrance.
Let dusk fall on burials shoddy mound.

I can tell you I love you

They take me to prison
With the lies of drugs
And they tell me not to rage.

But I will be.
In time the smallness will pass.
The cold bed. The evil of mockery.

I live in the minds of others.
I despise their pity
And their conformity.

I can tell you I love you

I didn't believe it

Crazy in the moment
Passive anger eats me.
I don't understand the future
And I need to hide.

The mind deserts.
Thought is unnecessary.
I knew this was coming.
I just didn't believe it.

I don't know what will happen next

I don't know what will happen next
Perhaps, guided by the hand of fate,
The strangers will disappear
and the friends remain.
Perhaps time will separate the wheat from the chaff
and we will again drink in the Kings Head
Knowing that we are the children of history
and this is our century.

I live gladly

The lady wishes to know
Have I ever contemplated suicide.
She asks with earnest intent
Cajoling me to respond as I will.

No. Life is too sweet,
The chances of a happy day too close.
Those I love are just too good to miss.

Let me breath longer
And live to see a ripe old age.
Though life's purpose is a mystery to me
I live gladly.

I love you

Words are free
But they cost the user.
A thousand mistaken phrases
Leave the lips
As each day passes.
' I love you ' is a case in point.
A hostage taken into captivity.
Will what is true today stay true forever?
Speak now and let the silence crumble.
A voice uttering the noble sentence
Is heard again.

I miss being me

I miss being me
I want to be myself.
I have not been myself
For quite a long time now.
Once I have conquered my demons
I will be on my way
Back to who I am.
There is hope.

I Record the Mind

It is verbal joy to write
To express the thoughts of being
I record the mind.
I mind the record.

I remember yesterday

Past times are me
I live in history.
My childhood is in my present.
I remember school and girls
And I dream of them now.

The tangled talk of the boy
Is in the man.
As time takes its toll
The past unfolds.
Driven into the future
I remember yesterday.

I Send My Message

I send my message
In an alphabetic guise
The code says I love you
The look of love
Is written down.

I sympathise with Oscar Wilde

I sympathise with Oscar Wilde.
What a price to pay for buggery.
The wit of the world
Snuffed out by upper crust fools.

I think I've lost my mind

I think I've lost my mind.
Looked for it behind the sofa
But it wasn't there.
I think its with my keys and phone;
Lost in space.

I think I've lost my mind.
Can't find it anywhere.
How shall I direct the search?
Who is in charge
Of operation brain.

I think I've lost my mind.
Gonna buy another one.
Look up minds on Amazon
And get a replacement
I think I've lost my mind.

I Wake

I wake to find the circus still in town
the sick clowns performing
the MC an egotist.
They recommend yoga to combat the actors
but this performance is a farce.
Insanity welcomes those with hating minds.
Fools prowl and the strongest survive.

I Write Love

I write love
And I mean love
Love now
Love tomorrow
Love forever
(or as much of forever as I am given).

If I Heard Voices

If I heard voices
Would they be singing
I hear the beating drums
I hear the astonishment of the keyboard
And I hear the accompaniment of guitars.
Is this a delicious insanity?

If You Could Read Between the Lines

If you could read between
love
the lines.

If Your God Gave You All You Wanted

If your God gave you all you wanted
Would you realise you had it?
Would you stop wanting more
And say I am happy forever?

Illicit thoughts

Like the Catholics of Elizabethan England
I look for fellow travellers in the crowd.
The illicit thoughts suppressed by the crown and its apparatchiks
Fill my head as I dream of freedom.

Like Shakespeare and Milton I know how it is to cross the powerful.
We only have our pens to lift our hearts.
England was built by dissenters.
Change only comes when the upper class is challenged.

I'm gonna shit on you

I'm gonna shit on you
Whatever you do.
Don't ask for mercy.
You didn't show any.

I'm great

I'm a better photographer than Shakespeare.
I'm a better recording artist than Newton.
I'm a better blogger than Einstein.
I'm great.

Immortal lines

I'm biding my time.
Waiting for an immortal line
Or two
To pass my way.
Sat on the bog
In silent vapour
Using paper
That would be better used
Wiping arses.

Imperfect Bodies

Imperfect bodies driven by lust
Bellies wobbling with each new thrust
The ardour of the middle-aged
Revived by the wish of a gnomic sage.
What was will never be again
But honest endeavour is our phallic game.

In the silence of the night

In the silence of the night
The mind is still.
After the day's hustle
The quiet speaks.
The darkness exudes its charm;
Now is the hour of contemplation.
In nocturnal thoughts
The brain slips free of its vicissitudes.
Now the turmoil subsides into sleep.
In slumbers realm the tiring day is released.

In the shadow of the church

We live our lives
In the shadow of the church
A generation that has moved on.
We still try to love our neighbour
But we refuse the hymnals song.

God is dead
But his spirit lives on
In the benevolence of the heart.
Jesus tried
But times change
This is atheisms start.

Infinity Beyond Infinity

The infinity beyond infinity
Fills the mathematician's mind
Twisting the fibres of extended grey matter
Into the matter of madness.

Irish Hymns

Irish hymns
And Irish hers
Are my new life.
I drink in Temple Bar
Sipping Guinness with the best.
I read about the Sistine Chapel.
Michaelangelo faced east and changed the world.
I faced west and changed myself.

Its only ink

Pen of pleasure
Write me a poem
Of joy and exhilaration.
Bring good times to this paper.
Bring a day of happiness
To my life.

Pen of pleasure
Its only ink.
Do you think
That this is to be my day?
I dream of excitement
Let's away to neverland.

It's Raining

It's raining
What a pathetic fallacy.
He can't get it up
What a pathetic phallusy.
She sucks
What a pathetic fellatio.
He can't sink a duck in the bath
What a pathetic Horatio.

Jerusalem

Oh William Blake
Though your words have majesty
You made a mistake
With the poetry of fire.

We don't want Jerusalem
On English soil.
Its full of Jews and Arabs
Filled with hate.

Fire your arrows of desire
Into the English
And bring us cosmopolitan life
And freedom from God.

John Hampden

I read a biography of John Hampden
As I languished in the psychiatric hospital.
I read of his learning, his bravery and his honour.
I read how this man of Buckinghamshire
Fought against tyranny
And resisted those who believed they had a divine right.
I see his statue
Standing boldly in the Market Square
Pointing a finger at the shame of this town.
I am a son of his house.
I believe in his cause.
I hope I live long enough to shaft the king.

Jupiter

Jupiter skylight of a winters night
Hang rock steady in the black.
Constellations mark your wanderers path
Beyond the sun and back.

Moons spin as Galileo saw,
When the Pope was made a liar.
The volcanoes of a lesser world,
Spew lava's molten fire.

The endless motion too will end
Far beyond one man's life.
Travel on stormy gas-world ball
Till your end in cosmic strife.

Late night music

Late night music.
I escape into the beat.
In the riot of sound
I am.

The hi-fi is my life.
One more C.D. before I die.
What will it be?
Paul and Bob are my destiny.

Dark shaking air fills the room.
The sound vibrates.
My ears feel the sublime.
What of Buddy and Eddie?

May this night never end.
May silence never descend.
One man and a guitar
Is all I ask.

Leave me alone

Leave me alone
I want to be grumpy
Like Van the Man in his Irish lair.
I don't want to live in goldfish bowl either.
I don't want to mess with fortune and fame.

I want to sit in my early dawn house
And watch the birds fight for peanuts and seed.
I know their only true allegiance
Is to the battle for sustenance
And the nestlings they feed.

Let me live

One day you are sitting in the sunshine dining a la carte
The next you are hearing bad news from the doctor.
Between now and then let me live.

Let the trees grow old

I no longer wish
To decide the fate of trees.
The noble beings
Outlive the navvies if left alone.
Chainsaws are the tools of hate.
Let the trees grow old.

Lie-bore scandal

The painter is a lie-bore scandal
Failing to strike the right balance
Between missionary zeal
and the mechanics of monetization.
With help he could graduate to be a real bee
We are bleeding darling
Not a bleeding saint.

Life and death

Born to die
And don't know why.
Three score years and ten
Of breathing gas and then
No more.
The flesh pumps blood
Until an unhappy ending.
Perhaps the point is to reproduce
Until eternity.
To be, oh yes, to be.
Ask your sons and daughters
If they are grateful
For their existence.

The grandchildren of the lineage
Will bring new life.
A baby lives without questions.
In the infant is the man.
From cot to cemetery is all there is.
The living years,
One life,
Fleeting youth
Leading to the coming end.
There is only one fact;
Death.

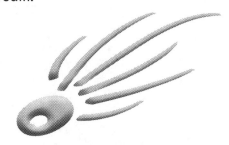

Life nags

Life nags like an addled tooth
Surly in discontent.
Is this all.
No more than this.
No better tomorrow.
There is no hope beyond living with disaster.

Life's lessons are hard learnt.
Beware of comfort
It softens the brain.
Beware of losing love
It brings only pain.
Beware of paradise
You're lucky if it lasts a day.

Life nags like an addled tooth
Surly in discontent.
Is this all.
No more than this.
No better tomorrow.
Three is no hope beyond living with disaster.

Like a lamb to the slaughter

Like a lamb to the slaughter
I fell in love.
No thought of the consequences.
It was a biological urge
I could not resist.

With soft kisses and a warm embrace
You plundered my heart.
I am amazed at my engagement.
My mind is rapidly melting.
Amorous intoxication fills the day.

Live now before times final call

Late night views of darkened windows
Capture the minds distraction.
Where sleep is denied
The electric light shines on.
The clock tells its early morning story.
In this room one man sits
And contemplates the world.
Four walls between the mind and the universes totality.
The fish and fowl live on in distant places.
Around the world the dawn spins in perpetual motion.
Wait for tomorrow and deny the tired moment.
This is all life has to offer.
Live now before times final call.

Live simply now

Seven billion beings
Pour out pollution by the day.
Carbon dioxide abounds.
Planes and cars and power stations
Take their toll on the atmosphere.

If a warmer world
Is to defeat my children
Can I say I was on holiday at the time
Guzzling gas in foreign climes?

The television talks of six degrees
And we all partake in conspicuous consumption.
Will city life bring mankind to its knees.
Live simply now
So the future doesn't kill us.

Locked In

Locked in
With the world locked out
Our bodies play a physical tune
Of love revived.

I write your name in air
And blow a kiss
And think of how best to spend
The moments of afterglow.

Tea and toast for the post orgasmic pair
Dressing gowns and slippers
We talk of the day ahead
And settle back to normality.

London

The train takes the strain as London approaches.
The cosmopolitan hub of the south.
The home of actors, artists and musicians
The city beckons by word of mouth.

Here you will find all of life
The rich, the poor and the crazy
Here you can work, scheme or dither
Or indulge your wish to be lazy.

The streets hold all the answers
Here the ruffians mix with the cream
Look in corners of the cities expanse
And it will fulfil your dreams.

Lost in the crowd

Lost in the crowd
An atom of being.
An individual surrounded by the many.
This is London.
A host of people.
I'm anonymous in the throng.

Love thy neighbour

Is it possible to love your neighbours in suburbia
When the kids shout and the lawnmowers roar.
The smoke from the barbecue is affecting my eyes
And we're arguing over the fence.

Think again Jesus
My neighbours are reclusive losers
We don't even see eye to eye
Over the positioning of the wheelie bins.

Market day in England

Its market day in England
The clustered stallholders hustle.
They sell the staples of life
For instant ready cash.
An open purse will bring you
A full and happy belly
And your due and deserved share
Of the fat of the land.

Masonic Bullies

Threats of abandonment and excommunication
Are repeated.
Intimidation resounds.
We will blackball you if you talk.
Speak not of masonic misdeeds
Or the forces of conformity
Will crush your social deviation.
With the authority of an unelected rabble
The bullies connive.

Masonic bums

Don't mess with me masonic bums
Or I'll spill the beans to the press
I've got a chip on my shoulder the size of a house
After eighteen years of duress.

Your sneering, sniggering, smug ways
And your belief you are better than me
Has left me with a raging loathing
I want to hang you all from a tree.

Mervyn Peake

Mervyn Peake of Gormenghast
I humbly salute your power.
Titus Groan and Titus Alone are immortal creations.
Your poetry bellows with elegant ardour
As I discovered in a twisted sunny hour
Although you went the way of mortals
You bring vivid joy to the living.
You observe the human pantomime
And brand it with divine comment.
You must have raged inside
To emit such fire.

Momentum, supremacy..............

Momentum, supremacy, Andalusia, division.
Vacation, hegemony, Croatia, incision.
Imposter, oligarchy, Malaya, interruption.
Pyjamas, kangaroo, New Guinea, assumption.

Callipygous, thaumaturge, Honduras, oblivion.
Steatopygous, idiot, Mexico, obsidian.
Ulitrichous, diagonal, Alaska, infection.
Mushy, ephemeral, Siberia, dissection.

Melleagrine, dissonant, Borneo, elation.
Divorce, dispersal, Botswana, generation.
Riperian, exceptional, Bolivia, micturation.
Dastardly, dental, Barbados, separation.

Divisive, disgust, Danzig, disorder.
Bivouac, bigamy, Bavaria, border.
Enliven, evolve, Estonia, espouse.
Subtle, sensitive, Slovakia, slouch.

Mortality

Church bells.
Farewell
To another man.

Prepare for death
As you draw breath
If you can.

This time
The chime
Is not for you.

But soon
The tune of doom
Will ring true.

The call of dying
Is not trying
To shock.

Mortality
Is mere banality.
You can't beat the clock.

My line lives on

I see my nose in the grandson's face
My daughter has my eyes.
Cast down the generations
My line lives on.

A jaw bone here
An eyebrow there
Cheating the unyielding clock.
My line lives on.

Half me and half my wife
The children live;
Their faces carrying selfish genes.
My line lives on.

My Mind Will Change

Is this a temporary sanity
Or a temporary madness
I don't believe in a steady state universe
My mind will change.

Night time

Grey shadows line the ceiling's width,
Moonlight passes the curtains edge.
The night time room is darkly quiet
Starlight creeping in.

The sleeper tosses as dreams invade
And wakes as visions fade.
The nightly parade of people past
Gives way to conscious thought.

The door crack shows the street lights glare,
The wall receives its lines.
You must wait now til the coming dawn
The fearful nightmare gone.

Night

Light leaches from an evening sky
As silhouettes emerge.
The stars appear, a planet too
As night prepares its time.

Now fox and owl will prowl the woods
And the moon rise over the hills.
The clouds will hide its nocturnal light
As the darkness covers the earth.

By the hearth of night
The human race will warm its winter chills.
The hours til dawn will pass in sleep
The quiet black surrounding.

Nightmares

Afraid of dreams that fill the night,
I wait til the new light.
The dawn relieves the pain of the nightmares path
The confusion of disjointed thought that tore the dark.

The past surfaces in mental turmoil
Characters of yesterday reviewed.
The brain bubbles up its scum of dread.
Sleep leads to an agony in the mind.

Parents pass with somnalent regret
A family of horrors fills the moment.
The fights I fought, the wars I lost come back.
Half awake I seek a brief escape.

No place to stand upright

The masonic bitch from hell divorced me
And took my money to another man
She had the virtue of a slut
But also many friends in low places.

The secret creeps bring hollow sympathy
And the friendship of imbeciles
They ask me to sell out to the nonsense of the eye
The intellectual garbage of the mob.

They threaten to deny my freedom
And surround me with a covert listening crowd
There is no life beyond treachery
No place to stand upright in the throng.

Notes for a Final Poem

I have come to write
I despair of despair
Bury me with a smile.

Nothing has a purpose

Nothing has a purpose
In these the dull days of winter.
The grey skies deaden the mind
And I think of alcohol and sleep.
January days are short and cold
And January nights are long and colder still.
As the birds fight for life in frozen England
I dream of sunnier climes
Where the skin can soak up the vertical rays.
Dormant plants and leafless trees
Stand proud against the wind.
Twigs and branches bow in surging air.
Come spring and release the sap
Come summer and free us.
This season is the harbinger of gloom
Pass by and bring us leafy summers tune.

Nothing much happened today

Nothing much happened today.
What a lucky escape.
Thousands died in wars and famines
But not here.
Here the day passed slowly.

To proclaim no interest in events
When half the world fights or starves
Is a western luxury.
What is there to care about when all is well in arcadia?
Who is moved by foreign sorrows?

The peace of village life is a reassurance.
The postman was today's main attraction.
Walking the dog the greatest cause.
In the lanes the tractors came and went.
The sun shone on the cornfields today.

In country slumbers the people pass their nights.
In indifferent pleasures they pass their days
And now they are one day nearer to death
Nothing much happened today
But the clocks kept ticking.

November 2

The last yellow leaves cling to the trees
Despite the vigour of the winter wind.
On the lawn there departed brothers
Tussle with the rain.

The first snow of winter threatens
As the temperature plummets towards frost.
The stagnant grass begins its winter halt
As natures hibernates in torpid slumber.

The sky darkens as the long night begins.
A chill wind keens at the door jam.
Rooks hasten to a massed winter roost
Clouds, surging by, dim the light.

Fox and badger prowl in search of food.
Darkness hides the coming winter world.
The trees prepare for the long months of cold.
I sit by the fire and think of growing old.

November

The weak winter sun shines low in the early dawn,
Long tree shadows dapple the grey-green grass,
Dew dropped blades feel the air's new warmth,
The season settles as November days move past.

Trees wait out the months of leafless cold,
These are the short chill days and long dark nights,
Dormant seeds lie still in sodden mud,
Birds fly south to sun and warmth and light.

Fallen leaves lie damp in moulding heaps
Future frosts will bring an icy freeze,
Winter witnesses the earth's persistent spin
A year must bring days such as these.

Now Is Wow

Convolute the words of a tight drama
Say more with less
Describe the anarchy of the mind
This is divine torture.
Predetermined freedom
Atomic movement in the brain.
Electrical excitement
Now is Wow.

NZ Poem

In the land of the long white cloud
The white man's law allows
His cars and cows and many million sheep.
Sparrows and starlings abound
As the kiwis death knell sounds
Done in by cats and possums in their sleep.
Clear the forest for cross and crown
Axe the kauri and rimu down
Now the moari must heat his hearth with tourist dollars.
A hangi for the Chinese throng
A haka and a sailing song
A tongue exposed to shrieking stamping hollers.
So buy a teiki and away
Say kia ora and good day
A beer with mates and then we must be gone.
Air New Zealand rules the skies
Great to see you and goodbye
The relies leave the southern cross shines on.

October Girl

October girl your day has come; your man says yes,
Its time to walk the pew-lined aisle and wear the dress.
Your summer wedding has won your father's blessing.
Prepare the car and set six bridesmaids dressing.
The rings are bought; the family throng attend.
May this sweet day live with you till your end.

Old farts of England

Gamboling, prancing old farts of England
Morris dancing on the village green
Circling, hopping, bending, bowing
In awe of the church and our Windsor queen.

What survives is what we wish
We take from the past what we choose
What carries on is today's survival
The worthless and old we lose.

Old

Housed in homes for the vacant aged
The demented parents pass their days.
Eating, shitting, farting, snoring
Waiting for deaths call.
The abandoned spouses savings bleed
Into bills for care and keep.
Time takes the final years,
Active life a memory.
Glazed eyes of mindless torpor
Issue out their fading call.
Who am I? Who are you?
Am I too old to live today
Or just too old to count the days
To oblivion.

On this day I lived and loved

The subdued light of evening
Prepares me for darkness and the death of the day.
In a final flourish the birds sing evensong.
The sun sets in fading cloud
As the first street lamps shine.
The sound of raucous jazz drifts from the house
As I go inside to say goodnight to today.
On this day I lived and loved.
What of tomorrow?

Ouvret la porte

I used to be a door
But then I became unhinged.
Ouvret la porte mon ami.
Mon Dieu.

Pass the Time

Although I am reluctant to write
I think the time has come
To make a mark on paper.
I have never suffered from writers block
And this is proof
I can write crap to pass the time
And you will read it.
Sorry I didn't mean that.

Payback

Stay back its payback
Revenge in the House of Commons.
Let the beads of secret sweat
Adorn the foreheads of the masonic mighty.
The herd will become thinking individuals
When the shit hits the fan.

People Watching

People watching
From the window of fate
Do the crowd wish to hang themselves?
Say thank you for today
And walk on by.

Picnic

In summer meadows I picnicked with my love.
The lark sang
And in the greenwood the song thrush burst forth with plangent calls.
On the grass we ate.
The brook burbled its endless tune
And all was well.

Now love has passed
And the grass has grown many times for hay
Since we spent our sunny afternoon in revery.
Now all that remains of our repast
Is the water's continuation
And the musk of a dog-fox.

Play on

The electric music beats,
Speakers transmitting sound.
Guitar and drums produce a sonic event;
The spirit of the times made loud.
A voice and a microphone
Tell of today's heartache,
Speaking of the mind's passage.
The ear receives the vibration of travelling noise.
The art of sound fills the brain.
A song speaks.
Play on.

Poetry

Write woven words
And leave your mark.
A book of poetry that lives on.
Proof to your descendants that you had a mind
And lived through pain and beauty.

The verses of sorted language
Will explain your generations thoughts.
In times to come
It will be the only proof of your existence
The only evidence of the brain's struggle.

Pottery

Moulded clay, manually kneaded
Adorns the fence
In multi-coloured ranks.
Ancient gods and oriental devils
Jostle with the abstract and the geometric.
Influences from Euclid to Picasso
Inform the ceramic show.
From the Ashmolean to the British Museum
The assembled faces bring their derivation.
The blue punk and Nefertiti gaze down upon the garden.
The gifts of the kiln hang on driven nails.
The visages of the imagination
Are my creation.

Prepare to fly

The airport lounge is full
With people who wish to be somewhere else.
Passports please,
Boarding passes ready.
Prepare to fly.
The sky beckons,
Take wing today.

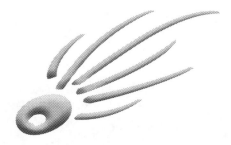

Provence provides

Provence provides le pain
Provence provides les croissants
Provence provides le cafe
Everything for a bonne petit dejeuner
In the sun

Provence provides la pate,
Provence provides le vin,
Provence provides la fromage,
Everything for a bonne repas
In the sun.

Provence provides la paysage
Provence provides la mer
Provence provides l'art
Everything for a bonne vacances
In the sun.

Rain beats on speckled glass

Rain beats on speckled glass
As the wind pushes its wetness to a smear.
This is an English spring.
The swallows cower.
The temperature plummets
As yesterdays sunshine becomes a memory.
The dandelions close
As a truculent evening sets in.
The birds forget to sing
In this seasonal demonstration of the weathers power.
May May become June
And not too soon.

Ray

Ray gaze at us with big brown eyes
As your life rises new in a new world.
Gaze at the colours of brilliant sensation
As you lie surrounded by the love of your family
Happy to see you and your personality unfold.
As we decline we pass the baton to childhood's star
Run fast and run true with the dreams of youth
And carry our line to a new century.

Red and yellow

Red and yellow
Blue and green
Stains brushed onto the white
Of virgin canvas:
Sent to do battle in a war of light.
One splodge or two vicar.
This is my mind mangled by the spectrum.
The palette of colour
Invades a 2-dimensional rectangle
And records the hope of a fearsome beauty.

Retirement

What to do with what is left.
Retirement beckons.
But there is no retirement from the poet's cause.
There are always more words.

More words to rearrange.
More sentences to be served.
I'll spend my pension on pen and paper
And age to the sound of new verse.

Right Now

I want it right now
I want it wrong tomorrow
I want it write now
I want it left tomorrow

Running on Empty

Are your days running on empty,
Or are there only ten left,
Or perhaps you will have a lifetime of joy.
The packaging of your heart will decide.
The clots will choose
If your brain is to have a future
Without hindrance
And if you are to be happy.

Sadness is impossible

How to live a life fulfilled?
How to negotiate the routine of passion?
The simplicity of a shared meal.
The ardour of a night of love.
How to? How to?

You wore that dress for me
And I know your heart.
Venice beckons.
I have known your love
And sadness is impossible.

Sectioned

A coven of witches section me
Believing in their sisters' rights
Lying women cover up female abuse.
The rights of man are dead.

Sedition has been made easier

Sedition has been made easier by the rise of the internet
A billion uncontrollable P.C.s are linked on line.
The secret world is now easily busted.
Julian Assange for president
And fuck the governments lies.

Self portrait with loathing

Six colours in plastic pots
Are what I have to express my grievance.
Blue and green,
Yellow and red,
Black and white;
Brushed on with intensity.
The shapes of my mind
Extended on canvas.
A rainbow cascades into view.
Self portrait with loathing becomes the day.

Separate from the Voodoo

Separate from the voodoo
I believe that the golden cross
And the tick on the forehead
Lead us nowhere.
I believe I have the strength of mind
To control my destiny.
Twice round the roundabout is unnecessary.
I control my fate
As much as anyone can.
In a random universe.

Shakespeare

A million combinations of words.
A jumbled dictionary saying just what you want to hear.
The precise selection says just that.
The mot juste speaks out.

The arrow of meaning pierces the air.
Language is the game.
The vocabulary of definition leaves the page.
Write what you will. Will wrote it before.

Silence the whistle blowers

Silence the whistle blowers
With dirty tricks.
Cover up the cover ups
And repeat the party line.

The old boy's network rules
Thanks to its following of fools.
They think they have the right to break the law.
It doesn't apply to them.

Masonic bums occupy the town hall.
The taxpayers pound is theirs
To share amongst the corrupt.
Save us from the brothers of the lodge.

Sitting doing nothing

Sitting doing nothing
the jailers suffer a mental block
Czech or check mate.

Sleep creeps

Sleep creeps behind my eyes
And tries to embrace me.
The pillow awaits the head.
Instead another cup of coffee
Keeps me awake.

For the sake of rest
I jest at the armchair.
A blanket and a cushion will be tonight's friends.
A perturbed mind is no accompaniment
To slumber.

Smokey's art is sublime

Swept away in the music of America
The songsmith's work envelopes the ear.
This is motown
And the moment of a sensitive love
Encapsulated in sound
Talks of beauty.
Smokey's art is sublime.
An album of rapture
Is my delight.
This disc is pure pleasure
Pure lyric divinity for the mind.

Snoring for England

I'm snoring for England
Crashed on the sofa
Drinking the dregs of a bottle of wine.
I'm feeling quite comfy
The music is playing
This evening I'm doing really just fine.

Snow

Snowy whiteness in the wind
Swirling flakes of frozen water
Touch the face of the crowd
And melt.
On this winters day
The ice debates its future with the sun.
The fields fill to a depth of white
And the rivers carry their full load to the sea.
The ridged roofs hang heavy
Bearing precipices of precipitation.
Fall, fall twirling snow
Cover the earth with pure coolness.
Fall, fall till the birth of another sunrise.

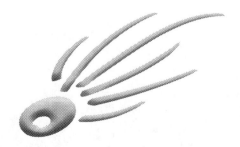

Solomons Decision

If Solomon's decision
Had never been made public
Who would have known of his wisdom.
The knife and the baby
Would be unremembered.
His reputation would not exist.
Who else would be a role model
For judgement.
Is there a modern man
Fit to fill a modern myth.

Someone to love

Sons and daughters are a solace,
Their loyalty one of life's great rewards.
The visits and the phone calls
Are the stuff of family ritual
And the grandchildren are the hope of the future.

My children, now adults themselves
Live and work, marry and cohabit
And continue with their descendant's destiny.
Their lives of youth pass with the days
As mine passes too.
I am thankful for their existence.
They are my someone to love.

Space time is mine

Space time is mine
As the galaxy drifts
Star by star
Towards armageddon.

Light years away
Light bends
Another galaxy shares its existence.
We gaze in awe.

As man's puny rockets explore Mars
Alpha centauri beckons
And the black hole at the centre yawns.
The children of stardust know no limits.

The super galaxies in the dark
Suggest infinity.
The saddle of space
Reaches back to the big bang.

Light that travels for a billion years
Tells us all.
This is eternity
In a moment.

Spanish coffee

The afternoon winds down
The lunchtime drunk
Has another coffee.
In foreign climes
Time is no stranger to disorder.
One more sip will right the ship,
Right the wrongs of the day.
Spanish coffee is good.

Spanish Holaday

Hola! Dos cerveza
and chips.
Would you like a postcard?
I'll sell you the stamps.
Aseos por favor.
We are the tourist tribe
Pissing for England.
Apologising for the Duke of Wellington.
It really wasn't our fault.
Don't forget to see Espana
Behind the cathedral wall.
The coach awaits.
We are driving over Spain.
Back to the hotel.
Back to back.

Spring

Spring follows winter
Like a pilgrim follows the lord;
With a certainty that only the weather can fake.
Bees and butterflies ring the changes.
The frosts retreat.
Buds are pent in their coming motion
The season of leaves is here.
Come summer warmth
And embrace our pale skin.
We wish for the sun
And the sun responds.

Suck Justice from the Sky

Suck justice from the sky
The dream of decision
Is on its way.
This is the night
Of black humour
Learn more and thrive.

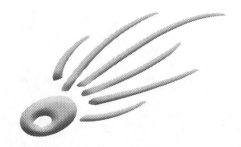

Summer Bees

The bee needs the flower,
The flower needs the bee,
This is how flowers should be
And bees should flower.

Nectar and pollen from the petalled interior
Carried to the comb on sunlit days.
This is how honey should be
Sugared product of a sweet smelling flower.

The worker visits the clover
And sucks the bending head.
This is how summer should be
The union of industrious insect and fragrant flower.

Summer dawn

The eastern horizon lightens in summer's dawn,
The wide sky brightens over hedge and hill,
The spinning earth brings another day.
We must fill the precious hours before winter's chill.
Make hay before the season steals away,
Make more of the time that is coming and is left.
The loom of life is ageing in its mill,
Time's fabric is summers warp and weft.

Summer Rain

It's raining again,
The garden rejoices,
The thirst of flowers
Pent up during parched hours
Gulps in the wild water.

Drops beat hard
On leaves and stems.
The summer storm brings relief.
The sky cries
And the earth smiles.

Fruits swell
The sacred drops nourish.
The cracked earth heals.
The clouds bring dark hope.
A damp life continues.

Summer Sun

Curved sweep of summer sun
An hour after dawn
The slanting rays heat and greet the lawn
A shadow moves as the minutes pass
Another day of solar destiny
Shines on planet earth.

Sunshine gives you cancer

Laid by the pool
Soaking up the rays
A thriller in one hand and a cocktail in the other
The foreign bums tan.
Turn over and grill the other side.
The hotel pool shimmers
And a fat German splashes.
The sunshine world attracts the tourists.
A line of parasols shades the poolside.
Put suntan oil on up to the bikini line
And doze away the day.
But never forget God's little joke;
Sunshine gives you cancer.

Swallow the sky.

You broke the world record
Without really trying
How much of the sky could you swallow
If you told the discus you hated it.

Symbolism stops at my door

Symbolism stops at my door
You can leave your eye in the trash,
The key and compass can go in the bin.
Your dogma has crashed with my karma.
I want no part of trowels and aprons
No nonsensical talk of performing art.
King Solomons temple is now defunct
The black and white floor is showing the dirt.
You've corrupted the nations police.
You've corrupted the houses of parliament.
You've corrupted local government.
Enough of this farce is enough.

Tall trees grow here

Tall trees grow here;
One hundred years without the saw.
Birds mate in their branches,
Caterpillars eat their leaves.
Columns of wood reaching to the sky.
The wind tests their strength.
The seasons watch their leaves come and go.
Lime and Ash grow old
Awaiting decay and disease.
Saplings shoot in their shade.
Will the saw allow them to grow tall too?

The Tap Drips

The tap drips
I complain about the plumbing
But we are lucky there is no flood.

Tell God what to think

Don't try and tell God what to think
He is an independent non entity
Circling in space on a loop tape
Pushing up the daisies.

He's also considerate to dandelions
and likes the odd buttercup
Roll him over in the clover
and hit him with your best marigolds

The A.A.

Arseholes anonymous
Will come to your rescue
If you breakdown
Or your car won't start.

They drive yellow vans
And wear yellow uniforms
And talk total shit
About the great architect.

The abandoned village

The abandoned village lies shrouded in undulating turf
The sward covering the mounds and humps of its destruction
All that remains of busy medieval life
Are lost walls and the business of archaeology.
The houses and streets now gone
Are grazed by a new population of cattle and sheep.
Where the yeoman of England once trod
All is now silence.
The lord of the manor lies rotten in his grave.
The peasants are forgotten.
Who could be an optimist when plague stalked the land
When the dead infected the living with bubonic extinction?

We live our lives in temporary towns
Aware that this is our fate too
We too will pass,
By a new plague or some impending disaster.
Our game will end.
We will be buried in accumulating soil
Our names lost in the passage of eternal time.

The Adjacent Man

Live in the now
And exchange tokens of goodness
With the people around you.
The past and future are a trap.
The news and the weather
Are a distraction from life.
Being kind to the adjacent man
Here and now
Is the best you can do.

The age of reason has passed us by

The age of reason has passed us by.
The blinkered self interest of the herd is all.
Care as long as it is convenient.
Charity allays the guilt.

The angels of solace

The conflict in the nation's heart
Brings forth the angels of solace
Those who choose not to fight
But to tend the battles wounded.

It is nobler to love your enemy
Than blindly support a warring tribe.
Why cheat your fellow man of his rights
When you can side with the cause of justice?

Pottery

The wheel spins.
The potters pot is spun to roundness
In hand-held ouze.
Wanting water and a skilled touch
The clay moulds in circularity.
A jug emerges.
From the geology of earth's sweet womb
The antideluvian art of pottery is reborn.
The kilns glow is a return to prehistory
Producing a tribute to man's longstanding ingenuity.

The Asylum

Dawn in the madhouse
The inmates stir.
Three hours yet till a breakfast
Of cornflakes and thinly buttered toast.
The medicated haze embraces the mind
As the dormitory curtains part.
The pyjamad shufflers piss and wash
To welcome one more day.
The kettle boils and tea brews
As gossip starts again.
' I own half of Microsoft'
And ' I can handle drugs.'
In the world of the insane
Dawn is the beginning of a new day of mundane madness.

The Average Delinquent

I am not particularly evil
I am the average delinquent
Standing on the spot
Waiting to know what to do next.

The barbecue

The fireglow light
Of tonight's barbecue
Dies slowly in the evening gloom.
A residual warmth
Cast around
As the embers fail.
Wine bottles lie injured on the lawn.
Plates and glasses stand
To see out the night
Until the morning.
Tonight we caroused
Tonight we ate, drank and made merry.
In summer's warmth
We talked away the night.
Farewell friends until another day
The stars shine down on your absence.

The beautiful survivor

Have you ever met a beautiful survivor?
Someone who made their way to today
Through the jungle's tangled thicket.
Recognise their worth.
They are an example of worthy persistence.
The triumph over tribulation that toughens the mind.

A life spent in existential battle
Leads to a knowledge of the self.
You may just be happy by the time you are old.
Content to die in the knowledge you have tried.
Somewhere on the path to today
You may have done something worthwhile.

The Big Apple

Will the Big Apple go the way of Apple Corps
Disputing the dollar on Wall Street.
Bankers whose reputations are surely sullied
Are toying with Madoff and his ponzi.

New York New York. Remember Enron.
You are only as good as your last deal.
The buck stops here
When the eagle flies on Monday.

The bigwigs are bending

The bigwigs are bending
The establishments crumbling
The weight of opinion is tipping the scales.
It won't be long before the tide has turned
And the lies of our rulers
Are finally nailed.

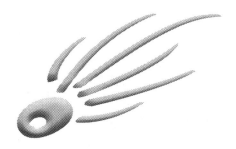

The birds of the air stand bedraggled

The birds of the air stand bedraggled
In this, another day of summer rain.
Hunched beneath the branches of ash and willow
They wait for a break in the cloud,
A chance to feel the broad sun beating on their back.

Pigeon and sparrow
Show the patient stoicism of wild survivors
As they search for food
On an overcast damp day of July.
They hope for a little of summers ease
Before the changing seasons
Bring the dark chill of winter.

The Black People

The black people have not learned their lesson
like the Jews they oppress the downtrodden,
climb the greasy pole
and discriminate.
Immigrants soon become a new enemy.

The blank page

This blank page is covered with vim and vigour
a cross section of my mind
A collection of the massives shame
As I watch the paint fade
This is one of the biggest contractual screw ups of all time.
We are bleeding darling
I feel like I've been a bullseye in an archery competition.

The bookcase

In stacked ranks
Stand a hundred books.
The product of a hundred minds
Dedicated to words.

The thoughts of this jostling throng
Carry me to distant shores and times.
Reading the lines
And turning the pages of skilled authors
Transforms life.

The day is better for a good read.
A book satisfies the minds need.

The cause

We don't care about your suffering.
We only care about ourselves.
The agony in your mind is a detail
And details are to be ignored
For the good of the cause.
We will treat you with bullshit and drugs
And carry on regardless despite the facts
However ridiculous the pretense.
We are sworn believers
And must carry on until the grave.

The chicken liberation front

The chicken in the supermarket
Led an unpleasant life.
Trapped in a giant shed
With a quarter of a million of its kind.
Deprived of a view of the sky
Or the chance to see the sun
It grew to adult size
In a life of eating and overcrowding.
This is no way to treat the living.
No way to prepare good food.
I've joined the chicken liberation front
Free the fowl and buy free-range.

The clowns of celebrity

Michelangelo and Leonardo,
The artists of the renaissance,
Blessed Italy's cultural heart
And left Europe richer.

We have Damien and Tracey,
The clowns of celebrity.
As they pile their cash higher
We know something has gone wrong.

The Coming party

With a sedative in one hand
And a stimulant in the other
I salute the coming party
With disbelief.

The crazy years of age

Golden grandson
Scion of the family tree
How great it was to be with you.
Now you crawl.
Now you laugh.
We dwell upon your every move.
The future is yours.
Time unravels in your favour.
I long to talk to you,
To see you walk.
The crazy years of age
Are yours for the taking.
Play with our dreams.
We worship at your feet.

The daisies are humble.

The daisies are humble.
Dicing with the mowers blade,
Awaiting the sun
Before their next mechanical beheading.
The flowers close to mark the coming evening
And, against a backdrop of green,
They open for the new day.
The children pick their chains
And where the blackbirds hop
The worms tunnel in the roots.
A thousand white survivors
Dapple the sward.
Such a simple beauty
Carpets the summer lawn.

The daisies dance with litter

By the blue fence
The daisies dance with litter
And the mind wrestles happiness

The Dawn

The dawn is the time poets love
Silence and the time to concentrate
As women balance the scales of justice
I ask for Roy Ayers and perfection.
The escape to Ronnie's was my beginning
Will this be the end

The devious county councillors

The devious county councillors
With their nods and knowing winks
Betray their shady allegiance
To the old boys club.

The millions of public money
Handled by these fools
Are supervised by the slimy
And handed to their friends.

Mend the roads and man the schools
With money from the taxpayer
And line the pockets of the in-crowd
The brothers of the lodge.

The distant window

In a distant window
A light burns even in daylight.
Be patient.
The mind's eye sees beyond
The wages of qualified fools.

The dream

Sleeps darkened room lies quiet.
Four dim walls surround the dreamer.
The nightmare runs swiftly through the nocturnal hours.
A cast of lovers past and dead parents
Appear in procession through slumbers oblivion.
The brain twists imagination.
The eyeballs move.
Another days detritus fills the void.
Sleep is here until the strained awakening.
The perturbed mind churns.

The drunken roundhead

I'm a drunken roundhead
Attending the theatre with my leveller friends.
Celebrating christmas
And eating the fatted turkey.

I shop on Sundays
And like a bit of stained glass
But any talk of Putney
Makes me want to cut off Charlie's head.

The egg in the nest

The miracle of the egg in the nest has been repeated.
The chicks have fledged and flown into the wood.
This years brood is alive and newly active.
The cycle of life and springtime birth persists.

The electric vigil

The late night light of the darkened hours shines on,
Glass reflects the image of the bulb.
Time passes as the clock labours hard.
The lonely hours of the nocturnal man unfold.

A minute takes an eternity to pass.
The lamplight glow beats back the engulfing gloom.
Tomorrow is another distant day.
Quiet stillness fills the dimmed, hushed room.

Shadows greet the dark adjusted eye.
Wait now for the night times passing muse.
The world sleeps with midnight now long gone.
The words of the electric vigil are coming soon.

The final couplet

Twee phrases and a simple rhyme
Coupled with a thou, thee or twas
Are not for me.
I prefer the exploration of insanity
And a harsh line.
The poetry of a debated madness
Brings with it its own language.
Paranoid schizophrenia is the charge.
Poets of a conventional form beware
In my condition the final couplet seldom rhymes.

The Fireball

The sun sets golden yellow
Dipping towards the horizon
In evening haze
The fireball drops
Beneath the houses of today's children.

The freedom of madness

The crazy leaps of mind
That take sanity away
Are living thoughts
To be celebrated
Along with the wild days they create.

The freedom of madness
Is a serious state.
In a riot of words and music
The brain enthuses.
There is no greater boredom than being sane.

The funeral in the rain

At the funeral in the rain
The black-clad throng queue
To throw a handful of dirt
On the human sod
Who for three score years and ten
Tormented his wife
And alienated his children.

Can we forgive his sins
As Jesus bullshits about resurrection.
We are all to be gone
Forever.
There is no going back.
If your life was shit
That's it.

The Funeral

The sun shone the day we burnt you.
We took your body in rented wheels
To the crem.
The crowd sang
And heard you praised
And then the fire raged.
We milled around until someone left
And others followed.
At your house we talked and drank,
Discussing flowers and charity donations,
Reviewing a life that was no more.
Your cat sat on your chair
As the mourners left.
Goodbye father.

The future explodes

Young mothers wheel the next generation
Up the high street and into the shops.
The infants grow daily towards their school days
The future of the nation emerges.

Who will be a leader of men
And who the recidivist delinquent.
Roll the dice of genes and nurture
And stand back as the future explodes.

The Game of Musical Standing

Who will be the last man upright
In the game of musical standing.
The hippy or the industrialist
The miser or the philanthropist
The sober or the seriously pissed
The on-target or the nearly missed.
I bet on the hippy.

The Garden

The worm abhors the light,
The birds friend.
The spade turns damp soil,
The weeds die young.
The chrysalis in the crack stirs,
A new insect risks life.
The gnats fly in sunlit clouds,
The swallows prey.
In a nest fledglings forsake the magpies gaze
And the crows murderous beak.
This is the garden.
A place of life and death,
Biological struggle
And perpetual hazard.

The gentleman of Rotary

I am a gentleman of Rotary.
I will not laugh at your indiscretions.
I will put you at your ease
And keep your secrets till I need them.

The God who doesn't exist

The God who doesn't exist
Wants us to be nice to each other
Without the bunkum of religion.

The Greek Tragedy

Was Beethoven's Ninth a fluke?
The EU anthem
Born of Napoleon's barbarity
Is still here.

The Greek Tragedy
Is not permanent
With a strong heart
They will rise again.

Aristotle is to be reborn
In the Athens of the south
Don't despair
The inventors of democracy will thrive.

The hall of echoes

In the hall of echoes
That is the mind at night
I wonder how to manage my condition.
To confide in the nurses
The nature of my delusions
Would be to admit error
But to pretend to normality
Would be to create a delusion in itself.
To speak calmly
Defuses the bomb that is paranoia.
I long for the morning
And sunlight
To shine on the mistakes of my mind.
A day of clarity
Must begin.

The heart of Brighton

The heart of Brighton wasn't built by the great architect
It was created by the average pen pusher
The buildings rise up from the pavement in disorder
As the inhabitants shuffle by

The home-town blues

How to escape the humdrum?
The same old faces.
The same old places.
How to escape?

Hard to thrill.
A lack of spice.
What is life's shape?
How to escape?

I've seen it all before.
There is nothing new.
I've walked these streets before.
How to escape?

The same old lies.
I don't know why you try.
It's the home town blues.
How to escape?

The injected life

As the mind rages
The words flow.
Dimmed by medication
The muse deserts.
The horror of insanity
Provokes a verbal response.
In the numbed state of swallowed tablets
There is little to be said.
The psychiatrists needle
Kills the poetry in the brain.
No words carry the day
In the injected life.

The Irish know, (on reading Ship of Fools).

The Irish know a thing or two
About how it feels to be ruled by fools.
They know the pillars of the community
Have their fingers in the till.

Naming names and exposing the corrupt
Is the necessary work of the newshound's day.
Hide if you can bent businessman.
The taxman owns your soul.

The Irish Mug

I bought myself an Irish mug
Emblazoned with a message
It talked of love and friendship
And was cheap at the price.

The jack of speed no.2

I used to employ the jack of speed.
He told me my home was Bedlam.
But my home will be where the kingfisher flies
There I will break the shape of the unknown.
Thank you Mr. Fagan.

The jackdaws chatter

The jackdaws chatter
In a March dawn
As a dripping drizzle covers the earth.
The windows run
And the glass roof patters.
In the sodden earth the worm stirs.
There is hope.
Spring comes and new life beckons.

The Jazz of Diversity

Is the jazz of diversity
Playing in the Joiners Arms.
Are the sultans of swing
In tonight.
Ronnie's is only a stones throw from Free Willy
Who will throw the first stone?

The jewellery of the sky

An evening star is out
The night is coming
Between the clouds a feint shimmer
Is the first of many.
The eye strains to see a distant sun.
The approaching darkness will release the multitude.
Come dark sky and bring me the stars.
The twilight is the harbinger of the milky ways splendour.
The time to gaze in awe
At the jewellery of the sky.

The king of number 23

A line of privet outlines the place
A car beside, the mark of the human race.
The drive is the beginning of the place to be
For me the king of number 23.

This is my gaff; my lawn, my house
I sit in my castle repelling louts
A British homeowner is the thing to be
I am the king of number 23.

I love this place, it is my own
My own true slice of the suburban zone.
Beware my dog and don't touch my tree
I am the king of number 23.

Watch out for the postman, he brings the bills
And the paper boy brings yesterdays ills
The letter box rattles with what is to be
The staple fare of number 23.

I live each day in suburban glory
The teller of a human story
When I die there'll remember me
As the one true king of number 23.

The knock on the door.

I fear the knock on the door
The ambulance come to collect
To take me back to bedlam
And lock me up again.

There is no hope against the doctor
No answer to medical law.
Who will protect the innocent
Before the masons call for more.

The Last Cuckoo

Buttercup stars shine in the springtime meadow
Aloft on stalks of green in the verdant sward.
Flowers await the mowers june tide anger
Vetch and clover spring with one accord.

The hawthorn hedge hangs heavy with mayflower blossom
Birds pipe their urgent evening calls
In a distant tree England's last cuckoo
Echoes in the dark of dusks decline and fall

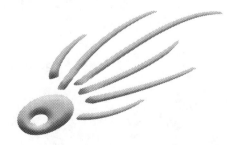

The Law of the Exceptional

The law of averages
Says you're different
Not the same as other fools
The law of the exceptional
Says I love you.

The lemmings

The lemmings are chasing after me,
I must not mention their name
Any mention of eyes and compasses
And they tell me I'm insane.

But its the duty of the intelligent
To speak with honesty
Lies and deception
Are not the way for me.

To be patronised by fools
Is a sad and sorry state
I want compensation
And the apology is late.

The lottery of life

Seeds hang from drooping twigs,
A generation yet to fall.
The fate of the species
Dangling in the wind.
The winter mud will receive the fallen germ
And spring will bring new life.
The survival of the fittest
Or maybe just the luckiest
Will see new leaves open to the sun.
Ten thousand chances for one new trunk.
The lottery of life.

The Lovesong of Tomorrow

This is the love song of tomorrow
Thursday will follow Wednesday
And I will kiss you.

The Lunatic Screams

The lunatic screams
I want it right now
But patience is a virtue
He'll still be mad tomorrow.

The M.P.s of Buckinghamshire

The M.P.s of Buckinghamshire
Aren't fit to lick John Hampden's arse.
There will be no statue
Of Bercow and Lidington
Put in the square
At the heart of the town.
The public life pygmies
Of the twenty first century
Will be remembered
For their deceitful lies
And their masonic dishonour.

The Madhouse Killer

The madhouse killer strikes,
The paper bears his picture.
Unforgiven and unforgotten
He punched a man and paid the price.
Another man, another day
And a bruise would have been the story
But for the madhouse killer bad luck is all.
He is put away to stew
On a life spent in asylums.
One violent night
When the temper blew
Determines the fate of the man.
A story in newsprint
Belies a double tragedy.
One dead, one locked up.
For what?

The minute

The clock moves forward another minute,
The red numbers read 1:47.
Around the world another thousand people die
And the sun ages.
The minute passes like a million before
But I see it pass
And remember how it is to lie silent in my bed
And see the clock count down the universe's demise.

The moment of elation

In a transcendent moment of elation
I see the bee suck the flower
And know that the bloom has fulfilled its purpose.
I rejoice to see natural destiny
Unfold before my eyes.
Could life be any better than to know
That my fellow inhabitants of the earth
Are living and breathing in unison
And know the pleasure of satisfaction.

The moment of flight

The pigeon on the fence
Began its day at daybreak
Spending the early hours of dawn
In search of another meal.
Its plumage freshly preened
At its belly full of corn
It contemplates its nest
And a clutch of new-laid eggs.
It spends today's time
Caring for its successors
And in the moment of its flight
Continues the fight of life and death.

The moon

Honey-glowing pitted skyball
Shine on.
Shine on through filigree bud bursting trees,
Thinning, splitting, branching.
Shine on through the phases of April, May and June
Til the haymakers moon hangs languid in the sky
Over silhouettes of darkened hills and spike-edged woods.
Shine on til the children play on browning lawns
In the endless end of summer's term.
Shine on through autumn's fall
When yellow leaves spin,
Twisting, twirling, dancing.
Shine on when winter nights bring frosted stars
And the waning crescent chases the constellations across the sky
Till dawns new day.
Shine on sweet skyball shine on.

The mother of parliaments

London is the home of two-faced parliamentary people
Smiling to the cameras
And covering up their deceit.
The principles of the elected are up for sale
As they cow-tow to their constituency bullies.
Stab justice in the back if it keeps you afloat.
Piss on the little man if it suits you.
Democracy has yet to arrive in England.
The mother of parliaments is a den of liars.
They only own up when they are caught
Until that day they rule us like cock-sure louts.

The Music has stopped

The music has stopped
But still the chairs rotate
Slamming doors are a chorus
Hide and seek is the game.
The retreat of the fatalistic is happening now
Freedom is.

The N.H.S.

We believe you are too elated
We'll give you drugs to make you less happy.
We are the N.H.S.
We'll use taxpayers money to deaden your soul.

The new day

A street lamp fades in the coming dawn
Paling as the minutes pass
The yellow light that pierced the night
Now dim before the sun.

The birds sing in the new day
Robin, thrush and dunnock.
With the easts light that cuts the night
The calendar turns a page.

Its time to begin again
To live the daily round
Breathe deep for life is new
And yours is yet to do.

Nightmares

The night twists and turns
Humdrum memories into nightmare illusions.
As the nocturnal hours progress
The mind develops its own array of familial delusions.

Waking in dread at what the brain apprehends
I retreat to a chair downstairs.
For coffee and the solace of waking
And the defusing of midnights cares.

Why the need to run riot in the imagination?
Why give credence to a forsaken past?
The thoughts of dawn will cleanse the nerves.
This night of torment won't be the last.

The Notes of Satisfaction

Sounds absorption
The staves way
Is the ears game.
I choose the music
And hope
To experience the new;
To be carried away
By musical enchanters;
To listen to the notes of satisfaction.

The Olympic Flame

The Olympic flame will come to Waddesdon
Travelling past the pubs and the houses
Asking the population to share its ancient ideals.
The runner bearing the fire of aspiration
Will pass by in a minute of transient truth.
As the traffic stops
The people of the town
Will have the chance to ask themselves
Do I share this burning of the heart?

The open door

This door may be trivial
It may be profound.
Embrace its possibilities
And enrich your life.
An open mind and an open heart
Will match an open door.

The orchid in the woods

The orchid in the woods
Is summers special gift.
By the ride of an ancient king
It grows in encompassing grass
Where the butterflies fly
And the bees thrive.
The stalk rises from the ground
Bearing a spike of colour in the green.
The spotted leaves soak in the light
To give life to the emerging flower.
The blue-white petals await an insects passing
As their subtle hue adorns the woodland scene.
The bloom will fade before the season ends,
Setting seed before the coming winter,
Returning to the earth from whence it came.

The pan fried dead

The big fish in a small pond plays dirty pool.
To swim with the sharks swim in armour.
To catch the local pike use live bait.
If you wish to eat your catch ask a chef to cook it.
Enjoy the flesh of the pan fried dead
But beware of the bones.

The past burns in

The past burns in.
Memories as urgent as breathe
From desperation revisited.
With hours that scored the brain we live on.
Carrying the weight of love
We are the children of the past
Reliving tomorrow.

The Past

History disintegrates,
Time unwinds,
Memory no more.
The people of the past fade into obscurity.
A generation drops its baggage.
Who are you?
Immortal lines are forgotten.
A century leaves its dead.
In infinite time nothing lasts.

The Photograph

A photograph of a smiling face
Lifts my heart
And gives me hope.
I am reassured that someone cares
And that there is some honour remaining in the world.
When I see your joyful eyes and mouth
Framed in squared wood
It gives me strength.

The poet of unparliamentary language

I am the poet of unparliamentary language.
I love to curse and swear.
With a shit, bugger, balls
I pass my time
For ' order order ' I don't care.

I don't care for the voice from the chair
And lengthy pleas for decorum
Bercow your a mason
A liar and a two-faced 'un
A man who knows how to bore 'em.

Bercow your a shit, a bastard and a git
A liar in life and in letters.
I long for the day
When crap like you is washed away
And your finally replaced by your betters.

The portrait

Paint dries
In subtle patterns.
A face conjured in oils
Adorns the canvas.

Look out dear sitter
You are recorded.
The colours of your existence
Are rendered.

The Practical Pacifist

I know I never started a war
I'm a practical pacifist
A soldier of verbal self defence
I call for a truce.
I have the shoes of Primo Levi
And the soul (?) of Goethe.

The Racing Mind

Will the racing mind win
Be lapped
Or surrender to the silence.
Throw the dice.
Virtue is all.

The Rain Falls

The rain falls
The daisies bend
By the green fence
Grass grows
The birds fly
And time passes
Another day of natural mystery
Is experienced.

The rain

The rain beats hard on the corrugated roof
Bringing its message of watery truth
The rivers respond with a dutiful surge
The soaked earth swells with a saturated urge.

The rain is the earth's wet salvation
Bringing its cleansing pure redemption
Wash away the stain of our mistakes
Bring the healing drops to this parched place.

The Red Lion

The newells of the staircase are ancient.
A million pounds was spent refurbishing the Red Lion
But the route to the loo remains the same.

The resistance

I'm going to take to the hills
And join the resistance
To fight the good fight
Against the agents of greed.

I'll camp in the woods
And polish my rifle
And deliver the peasants
From want and need.

I'll assassinate the brothers
And liberate the county
And install a regime
Of honest M.P.s

I'll blow up the town hall
And bomb bloody Tindal
And bring the establishment
Down to its knees.

The riot in the library

There's been a riot in the library
The books are fighting back.
Their fighting over the average reader
Fighting over the average hack.

The dispute in the nations heart
Will be fought out in ink
Words will decide the issue,.
Words will cleanse the stink..

The Rose

Faded rose, a curled impression of what once was,
Your perfume spent,
A scent of passed days,
Your short life graced my window.
Now new buds follow,
Opening to the sunlit sky.
Why is beauty brief?
Why do flowers die?

The sentences of now

A pen and paper
Record my thoughts.
The words of the mind
Are committed to physical form
By the alphabet in ink.
In this early morning
I sit and write
And gaze through the window
At the waking world outside.
These are ruminations
Of the living brain,
The letters and words
Of today's existence.
The sentences of now.

The Sign at the Entrance

The sign in the car park
Says live at your own risk
What does it say at the entrance.

The sky promises

Flowers stand open to the driving, teeming rain
Petals battered by the falling downbeat of the drops
The crimson and ochre blooms of summer
Carry liquid beads of translucent dripping moisture.
The damp drooping heads bend beneath the weight.
The coming buds resist the insistent downpour.
Roots absorb the nourishment delivered from the clouds.
The sky promises more refreshing deliverance.

Without this there would be no roses,
No chrysanthemums, no margarites,
No floral profusion in the garden of June and July.
Let the summer rain cascade down on the pots and borders,
On the window-framed view of leaves and vibrant colours.
This necessary soaking of the soil
Will bring more months of summer plenty
And revive the stems and stamens of a passing season.

The Son of a Hero

The son of a hero
I call for an encore
Lead me to humility, liberty and decision.

The song of summer's coming

The dawn chorus sounds,
Chiff-chaff on chaffinch
Blackbird on blue tit.
As if singing for joy
The birds proclaim their territory
And seduce their mates.
In the spring dawn the sun rises
To the sound of music.
Sing songsters sing;
The song of summer's coming.
A day of nest bound toil awaits
So herald the day while you can.

The sorrow of silence

The sorrow of your silence has passed
I no longer suffer the pain of your betrayal.
The passing years have lifted the weight of family treason.
There is no more agony of the mind.

In time I will get even
And the hidden truth will be known.
I will not bear the scars of a bad marriage for ever.
Your petty loyalties will be exposed.

The triumph of sound

Violin and violas
Rage in unison
With a tympany and bass accompaniment.
This is the ear's delight
The sound of triumph.

The french horn and the trombone
Are united in music
With surging harp and singing cello.
This is the ear's delight
The triumph of sound.

The speaker of the house of commons

The speaker of the house of commons is vexatious and absurd
He has all the grace and dignity of a steaming poodles turd.
His mind of grubby secrets is a shame to public life.
I don't know whose the bigger arsehole him or his wife.

The statue of liberty

In New York harbour stands the French gift
Torch aloft in pale green.
A celebration of the departure of the English.
A statement of intent.

If America is to achieve liberty
It will have to get rid of the masonic bums.
The land of the tree is a slave to the cheats
Millions of losers clog its veins.

The sun is shining now

As the world turns
Seven billion lives unfold.
From birth to death
The days pass.

In sickness and in health,
How many are happy?
How many realise that this life
Is just a temporary aberration?

Grandpa breathes his last
As a baby cries.
The children of tomorrow look to the skies.
The sun is shining now.

The sun sets in the north

The sun sets in the north
Confused by its eclipse.
Falling below the evening horizon
It slides down the madhouse roof
Into a boiling ocean.
Gone.
Forever.

The testimonial of esteem

Dad hustled in the biscuit factory
Worked hard and got his hands dirty
But the wrath of mammon fell upon him
And took away his dream.
The testimonial of esteem and the salvaged scrap
Restored his fortunes.
He rose from the ashes
The phoenix of Slough
And lived a life of plenty.

The thieves of the mind

I cry like a fool
For the world they have taken
In the temporary home
Of the thieves of the mind.

The tide in the marshes

Born aloft by running dogs
I embrace the heraldic dawn of slumber
The tide in the marshes brings water to the door.
Clocks that ticked before my time
Remind me that the storm which made the trees dance has abated.
This day's beauty brings sunlight to the green meadow
And within four suburban walls
I sleep with magic.
The dream of rural splendour wraps the mind.

The tyranny of consultants

The tyranny of the consultants
With their array of legal powers
Is a fate best avoided
By those who wish to be free.
Their belief that they know best
And can guide their fellow adults
Is a grand delusion of its own.
A product of limited minds.
Psychiatry is no science
Drugs and diagnostic labels no solution
Suing the masonic arseholes
Is the only way to go.

The victims of psychiatry

A bond of friendship exists
Between me and my fellow victims of psychiatry.
Sectioned behind closed electric doors
We were united in our defiance of the regime.
Imprisoned without trial we prayed for medical mercy
And the passing smiles of the kinder nurses.
Now released we meet to eat and drink,
To discuss the wreckage of our lives.
We talk of our divorces and our estranged children,
Of medication and appointments with the quack.
Free from the repression and barbaric interference
We bemoan the day we ever became entangled with bogus medicine,
With masonic consultants full of lies and deceit.
A curse on you bastards for the theft of our liberty
And the sham doctoral certificates that put you above the law.

The village on the hill

Ancient pantiles line up
On medieval timbers
Preparing for the rain
Of a mediterranean winter.

We sip ' deux verres de vin blanc'
And bask in the autumn sun.
The clay ridges cascade down the hill
As the house tumble one on one.

The village on the hill
Spreads before us in slanting lines.
Time for a light lunch
And another glass of wine.

The voice of Tina Turner

The voice of Tina Turner excites me
Dusty Springfield ignites my mind
Cyndi Lauper brings out my true colours
Suzanne Vega lifts my heart.

Mica Paris brings me joy
Alison Moyet gives me strength
Nina Simone makes me want to fight for my rights
Ella Fitzgerald reminds me that there is grace in the human heart.

Women of the world raise your voices
I find solace in your song
My happiness increases with each golden note
Shower me the inspiration of your sublime music.

The vortex of the night

The grey clouds scud in ragged ranks across the dimming sky,
The silhouettes of churchyard trees bow as they pass by,
A crow flies in raging air and skirts its blowing dimensions,
Its wings ride the gushing tide with retractions and extensions.
The black feathers mock the night with dark anticipation,
This winters night the bird flies above the human nation.
Its lime tree roost awaits it now, a place of rest and quiet
The gale will blow in darkened hours, the vortex of the night.

The way home

Black air absorbs the glare,
The hooded lights hang;
Shining now before the dawn.
The amellioraters of the night;
The street lamps mark the way,
Alternate blazes of sodium yellow
Reflected in the pavement puddles.
Pools of luminescense light the path.
The nocturnal traveller passes by.
This is the way home,
Tonight.

The Whisper

You may have disturbed me
I may have been sleeping lightly
For some reason I was awake
When I heard you whisper his name.

The Wind in The Ashes

The wind in the ashes
Whispers Lindsey
The wind in the birches
Whispers Robin
The wind in the willows
Whispers Ray.

The wind in the willows again

The ashes leaders nod.
A windy dusk
Leaves leaves to bend.
This years twigs feel the strain.
(Grow or die
The trees motto).
As light fades the wind takes the lead.
Violent air surrounds the wood.
The wind in the willows again

The wordsmith's fate

The wage slaves commute
As the poet muses.
In the offices of the employed
The salaried hours pass.
In the literary den
The wordsmith spends his time
Rearranging the dictionary.
With the P.C. Screen and the cordless phone
The worker's day is passed.
How lucky to escape this commercial fate
And play with words.

The yaffle

The yaffle laughs.
Its probing beak pierced the summer lawn
As ants scurried from a chasing tongue.
The flash of green and yellow disappears
Disturbed by a man's sudden unannounced approach.
A trees shelter is the woodpecker's escape
The retreating flight glimpsed by an earth-bound ape.

The art of pottery

The wheel spins.
The potters pot is spun to roundness
In hand-held ouze.
Wanting water and a skilled touch
The clay moulds in circularity.
A jug emerges.
From the geology of earth's sweet womb
The antideluvian art of pottery is reborn.
The kilns glow is a return to prehistory
Producing a tribute to man's ingenuity.

They think their God is better

They think their God is better
But what do they know.
We've left God behind.
We don't find
Solace in medieval superstition.

The children of Allah
Will grow up as education spreads.
In their heads
Will grow a belief
That God is nought.

There is no God
In the East or the West.
Its taken us centuries to be rid of him.
We don't want this nonsense
Any more.

Thick trousers

I wear thick trousers
They can't see a woman coming.
They bend at the knees
But the thighs are a secret.
And when it comes to a belt
I'm anybody's.

This poem

This poem doesn't scan.
The man who wrote it didn't care
About the words of other scribes.
So let's scribble now in freedom
For to care too much what others think
Is slavery.

The average minnow rampant

The heraldry of ancient times is what is needed now.
I want a shield emblazoned with my emblem
To protect me in my battle.
My symbol will be an average minnow rampant
Gamely swimming against the current
And fearing the kingfishers dive.

Throw caution to the wind

Throw caution to the wind
And let the gale rage
There is no time for timidness
In this brief life.

Let the hurricane blow
And free you from inhibition
Summon up your strength
And face your share of strife.

Tibet

It fills me with anger
To see the Dalai Llama
Talk of happiness
As the Chinese take his land.
Buddhism preaches peace
But do the rulers of Beijing understand the word.

To David Jason and Jackie Stewart

When the showbiz folk have made it
They move to Buckinghamshire.
We were born there
Among the labourers and the scum
Amongst the housing estates of the common.
The home counties homes of the elite
Are mown by the plebs
And cleaned by the Poles.
We know you are only posing
As denizens of the Chilterns.

To Dine With Children

To dine with children
Is my idea of heaven
Innocent laughter
And innocent questions
Fill the air.
The sacred members
Of a coming generation
Share their presence.

To Hate a Stranger

To hate a stranger is perverse
How can you judge an unknown mind?
Are there no Samaritans in England?
The key in the door has been removed
Today I heard of bigism
The offence of losing in the battle of good against evil.

To live on

The sun has 5 billion years to go,
We have got to get out quick.
If we are the only ones experimenting with consciousness
It is our duty.
Explore the galaxy
Planet by planet.
Take off for the unknown.
Its the only way to live on.

To Ray

Caged in your bed,
Fighting the outrages of age,
I think of you.
May your spirit stay strong.
May your steady mind live on.

I remember your kindness
And your humour.
Like your brother you did not suffer fools gladly
But unlike him you live.
Stay strong. Live on.
Live on. Stay strong.

To Ray

New born Ray
Scion of the house of Osagie
And my first grandchild
Your experience of the world
Is but a few hours.
I wish you well.

May you grow tall and strong.
May you live to have children of your own.
May you be healthy, happy and wise.
You carry my genes into the future
And you carry with you my love and blessing.
Oh happy day.

To Read or Write

To read or write
That is the question.
To add another poem
To the millions that exist
Or suck the juice from Shakespeare
And await inspiration.

To see you bastards gone

The cloying hands
Of the children of freemasonry
Still chase me in my dreams
As once they chased me in life.

With the meddling of personal control
The seeds sown by a bent council
Grow still
In a parade of nightmares.

They believe that there is nobody or nothing that can't be fixed with a
bribe
No issue that can't be settled by men in suits.
The black tie, the penguin suit, the farce of ladies night
Convince them that they are respectable.

Bent fools plying their trade in the gutter
With their noose and their trouser leg rolled up.
Oh to see you bastards gone.
Oh to strike a blow for honesty.

To the freemasons

You robbed me of my livelihood.
You robbed me of my house.
You robbed me of my marriage.
You robbed me of my sanity.

You offered me no apology.
You offered me no compensation.
You offered me no justification.
You offered me no hope.

To Tommy and Pat

On foreign soil the lonely widow mourns
In the caverns of a fading mind.
To the husband, fallen in England,
The crematorium offers its flames.
This day marks a life ended
As a dream of Ireland awaits the ashes.
The sadness of a life disintegrating pervades the day.
There is no peace in the agony of ageing.

To William

There is no denying that I love you
After an absence of far too long.
No denying that I am sorry for your sorrow.
I long to see your face
And see the change that age has wrought
Before it is to late for me to see at all.
Come back, come back, forgive.
Let your heart give the love that mine is want to give.

Today is now

Dawn breaks on a brighter day.
Today I will pay off my debts
And break the logjam.
I will give blood and dine with a friend.
Today I will feel good.
Today brings the hope of something better.
Today is now.

Today the sky is dry

Today the sky is dry
the rain has receded
the riot in my mind
is controlled by willpower
I rage against polluted minds
persecution is in the air
John Donne brings the good morrow
and Mervyn Peake is perfection.

Today's earth

The world turns as I stand still.
Here before my birth
And continuing to turn after my demise.
Stuck to the surface by gravity
I inhabit the crust,
Between the earth and sky.
Walking over hill and dale
In a temporary human life.
My footprints are my legacy,
Shapes in the yielding mud.
My presence here is a temporal fact.
I exist in the only moment that is the present.
This is it.
Today's earth.

Turn off the lights

Turn off the lights
Switch off the cooker
You're killing the polar bears
And destroying the penguins.

Stop breathing out CO_2
And plant a tree
You'll be found guilty in the court of green justice.
Will your funeral be carbon nuetral.

Two hours after midnight

Two hours after midnight
Awake in the hour of nocturnal doubt
I gaze at the darkened ceiling
And wonder why we are so fragile.
The death of a friend leaves me to ruminate
On an insecure and temporary life.
A heart attack or a tumour away from extinction
With the doors of middle age closing
I ponder the passing night
And vow that I must live tomorrow.

Uni-verse

I came from an egg and a spermatazoon
Put on twelve stone clothes and two shoes.
I went to the pub, it was love at first sight,
Now my genes spiral out into infinite night.

Unparliamentary language

I am the poet of unparliamentary language,
I like to curse and swear.
I say what I want
Despite rebukes from the speakers chair.

Cameron can't say idiot
But I fucking well can
Bercow you're a buffoon
A mason without a plan.

Vegetable companions

As I sit in silence
Alone in this empty house
The trees grow
And the lawn sprouts.
The roses bloom
And the rhubarb reaches to the sky.
My vegetable companions brook no argument
They continue their photosynthetic movement.
They surround me with green life
Sharing my time
And relishing their existence.

Verse

Speak nicely of the poets verse
For it would be a little worse
If it were not made to rhyme
All the bloody, fucking time.

Waiting for the dawn

Waiting for the dawn
In darkened silence.
Waiting for the sky to lighten.
Waiting for the silhouettes of trees
To stand tall in morning air.

Clouds emerge in whitening translucense.
Birds stir.
In coffee and toast the days ritual begins.
Night is over.
Long hours of solitude retreat before the coming day.
In the half light time continues.

Washing the car and mowing the lawn

England is the only civilization
Based on washing the car
And mowing the lawn.
In the suburban streets
The middle class masses
Busy themselves
In the chores of the day.
Keep up with neighbours
Keep up appearances
Keep tidy and prim
And value the house.
The stripes on the lawn
And the shine on the car
Are testimony
To consumerist care.
With shopping by day
And watching telly by night
The lives of the many
Are ticking away.
Down at the golf club
They gossip and banter
And pass the time
Of another bourgeois day.
Vote for the Tories
And join the masons
Conform to the norm
And stay in line.
Wash the double glazing
Decorate the house
Is this the way
To spend your once given time?

Wat Tyler and John Bull

Wat Tyler and John Bull,
Heroes from another age,
Fought the duplicitous king
To make England a fairer land.
I wish I had been with them
To face up to the overweening monarch,
Bring medieval progress
And end the feudal age.
The change they sought in England
Is still occurring now.

Waves, flames and clouds.

Waves, flames and clouds
Are natures movement
Curling swirls of earthly motion
Riding the skies and tides of a churning planet.
The shapes of wood and water
Are summer showers and winter's flickering warmth;
The rhythm of existence made plain.
Rain and spray and a spitting log
Testify to the elements natural form.
The laws of physics deliver both harmony and the storm.
From the deluge to the bushfire
The planets surface celebrates its atomic freedom.
Move again earth mother, move again.

We are truly blessed

Thank God I met you
And the chance encounter
That became love
Wasn't swept away
By the sea of probability.

Thank God your smile
Struck my eye
And told me
That the time was now
And that you were the one.

Thank God we are still alive
Breathing in
The sighs of love
Knowing that our
One and only life is truly blessed.

What bollocks

Do you want to make my life a joke?
Make me a puppet of the local grandees?
Serving the local mafia
Cutting their hedges and felling their trees.

You tell me I'm ill because I can see through this nonsense.
What bollocks.
I'm starting my own non-secret society.
Its called the grown-ups.
To get in you must publicly avow your membership.

What do I need today

What do I need today
Content to be indolent;
Not hungry not thirsty
I want for nothing.

Is this stalemate contentment.
There is always more.
Can I be happy
Knowing I have everything.

What Do the Birds Do

What do the birds do
When we are not watching?
Do they talk in tongues?
Do they fly the sky.
In aerobatic formation?
Do they fuck and court with ritual immemorial?
I know they do this when I watch
What more is possible in my absence?.

What I thought in the womb

Why can't I remember
What I thought in the womb
My nascent mind was there
But my memory was not.

When Black hates White

When black hates white
As they were hated in their turn
We have come full circle.
To defend the empire with a symbolic potato
Is to cheapen the soul.
Tomorrow is another day of childish war
Their bullets are blanks
And the insults are from the school yard.

Whitney Died

Whitney died:
Not a wasted life.
The lucky ones stay off drugs
We live on
To hear your songs
We have learned from your memory.

Who is reading my words

Who is reading my words
The score on paper
The author is free to write
and to right.
Write the wrongs of freemasonry.

Commercial cheats are not to prosper.
Special pleading and privilege
are not the way forward.
Secrecy breeds corruption.
Masonic business is for the second rate.
Beware the mafia of the mediocre.

Winter fruit

Bananas and oranges from distant shores
Fill my bowl.
The world beats a path to my pantry.
The fruits of foreign soils are mine.

I eat the world
And the labours of countless children of toil
Provide for me.
Oh what it is to be born
In a time of plenty.

Lemons and mangoes are the barrow-boys friend.
The traders call their names.
Pineapple and melon fill their crates
It's never winter on the market.

Wiser than myself

The agony of irrational anxiety splits the mind,
These are the moments of self doubt.
The brain sees through itself.
Beliefs of nonsense
People the present.
I know my thoughts are false.
I am wiser than myself.

Wishes

If I could be anything I chose
I would be more of the same.
A better poet,
A better potter,
A better father,
A better lover.
A better photographer,
A better cook.
I would be physically fitter,
More charitable,
More supportive,
More loving.
But most of all I would be young again.
Back to then days when hope was bright
And the future seemed endless and limitless.

With W.B. To Innisfree

With W.B. To Innisfree
To visit the bee-loud glade
There he bade fight for the right.
The rights of man
And the right word.
And where the lake laps the sure
To bring a little uncertainty
To comfortable folk.
His Irish eyes smiled
As I told him of my quest.
And he spoke to me thus.
' No freemason is free
No freemason is sane.
A brain of stone needs cutting.
The separate tribe offer nothing.
Better the day they die.
Rave on R.C.
Don't let them tread on your dreams'

Without Me

I appeal to the alphabet
To tell the world
What it is like to be alive now.
Here I am nearer to death than birth
Passing my time arranging words.

As technology speeds towards a new generation
I type my plea on a dated computer,
Not sure which branch of electronics
Will seize the day,
I watch the facebook era pass by.

Medicine will make us live longer.
A demented old age beckons for many.
If I live long enough to receive my pension
I will brood on the passing of time
And watch my grandchildren live.

What will be their zeitgeist?
What world will they inhabit?
As time passes the world will change.
Tomorrow will be a new world
Without me.

Woman's hour

Oh woman's hour
You talk of patriarchy and thrush
And the liberation of the weaker sex.
Is my mother listening?
Does my wife care?
The recently caught diseases of the London crew
Are not the gossip in rural arcadia.

Women's Boxing

Women's boxing on tv today
A breakthrough for barbarism
Is it in a womans heart to put a fist in your face
Duelling was left behind with Victorian gents
Progress would be enlightenment and love.
NO.

Words are free

Words are free,
The dictionary is no secret,
So speak as you will.
The tongue of liberty is prized
Not to be taken by a dictators bullies
Or masonic fools.
Speak freely
For life is too short for lies.
The niceties of sophistry
Or the phrases of dumb ignorance
Are wasted time.
Voice the issues of your age
And do it now.

Write on

A pen records the words
Of thoughts production.
Ink on paper takes the message.
A nib carries all before it.
Write on.

X

X marks the spot Apples
Y you ask Bite
Z Children

You are no brother of mine

Oh brother of the eye
You call everyone brother except me.
With your cocaine deals and your financial fraud
You are an ideal member of the royal scam.
You stabbed your own kith and kin
In the breadth of the back
For the sake of some bums in the council.
You are no free mason.
You are a slave to this shit.
The polluted waters of your jaundiced mind
Are thicker than blood.

You took me in my diluted sanity

You took me in my diluted sanity
To see George Clooney weave his spell.
You loved him
But you loved me more.
As we gazed at the glory of cinema
We felt as one.

Your love is all

In the uncertainty of a mind consumed
All I know is that in the moment of your smile
My heart lived.
Tomorrow I will breathe
But who will bring the light of love to my door.
Oh voluptuous I long for a night in the bed of dreams.
You wore my necklace.
I shared your heart.
For now your love is all.

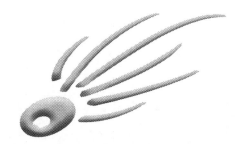

Printed in the United States
By Bookmasters